23.

9.

Both Sides of the Fence

Frank Cullum
BOTH SIDES OF THE FENCE

edited by Pauline Cullum

With Illustrations by J. M. Paley

Tyndale + Panda Publishing

Copyright © 1987 Frank Cullum
Copyright © 1987 Tyndale + Panda Publishing Ltd.

CONDITIONS OF SALE
This book is sold subject to the condition that it shall
not, by way of trade or otherwise, be lent, re-sold, hired out,
or otherwise circulated, without the publishers' prior consent,
in any form of binding or cover other than that in which
it is published and without a similar condition including
this condition being imposed on the subsequent purchaser.

First published 1987 by Tyndale + Panda Publishing Ltd.
117 High Street, Lowestoft, Suffolk

Printed in England by Tyndale Press (Lowestoft) Ltd.
Wildes Street, Lowestoft, Suffolk

Typeset by Anglia Repro Services
133 South Quay, Great Yarmouth, Norfolk

ISBN 1 870094 02 6

For Pauline

Contents

FOREWORD

by Nick Duval

I first met Frank Cullum at a formal shoot near Norwich some 14 years ago. He was then, and had been since the war, the professional gamekeeper he is. His advice, his comments before a drive, and his wit has made many a shooting guest feel at home and at ease.

Following the famous narratives of the '30's, *The Rabbit Skin Cap* and *I Walked by Night,* edited by Lilias Rider Haggard, stories of poacher come gamekeeper have always been popular with town and country readers alike. This new work is a refreshing reminder of how hard real country life was even 30 or so years ago. The village social life, the old characters and family dependence on full employment, coupled with everyday work in the fields and woods of Norfolk and Suffolk contribute to a fascinating biography of a 'keeper's tale.

I remember enjoying the splendid works of Richard Jefferies and W. H. Hudson of the late Victorian period. *Both Sides of the Fence* is an up-to-date revelation near to every countryman's heart — a story told with frankness, feeling and a wealth of experience.

Typical of the cunning countryman, when Frank was asked a somewhat difficult question at a shoot, he replied with diplomatic Norfolk caution, "It's all according." Such is the wisdom in the country of actually sitting on the fence. It is a pleasure to forword such a book, put together in a 'keeper's cottage in one long winter. Frank's concise memories are well and truly documented for ever.

Anglia Television
September 1987

11

CHAPTER 1

My Father

I was born two years after the Great War. My father survived this holocaust, serving the duration in France in the Army Service Corps and endured some terrible experiences. He enlisted as a lad of nineteen and returned home unscathed, a man of twenty-three. On his return to the village, after discharge, he found life rather mundane. After his wartime experiences, he could not face returning to farm work and within two weeks had re-enlisted in the Royal Horse Guards, the Blues.

He had no difficulty passing out as a cavalryman as he had vast experience with horses. During the war he was handling a team and prior to army life, it was all horses on the farm. He looked resplendent in his uniform, from his black, polished knee-length riding boots to his gleaming breast plate. Coming home to the village on his first leave, he had all the girls after him. Mother must have caught his eye, for after his return to the regiment, a lot of correspondence began to flow between the village and Knightsbridge Barracks. He was married during his next leave and eventually I became the first offspring.

I think my early days were very comfortable with Mother receiving army pay and, being the only child, I had all my mother's love and undivided attention. Two years later I was joined by a brother, and Mother began to play up, wanting Father to come out of the army to be by her side. Whose decision it was I know not, but I don't think it was a very good one in a business sense as unemployment was rife and the only work ever available in the village was farm work, which was very poorly paid. Anyway, Mother wanted him home with her and the family and to keep an eye on him — a little of each as Father was renowned for being a 'bit of a lad'. This came home to me when I joined the same regiment twenty years later. When all the new recruits were lined up in their civvies, the Regimental Sergeant Major marched down the line with his head held high, his stick under his arm and his chest out. After addressing the man beside me, he barked at me "What's your name?" I smartly replied, "Cullum, Sergeant Major". "Cullum! Wasn't your father in this regiment?" "Yes, Sergeant Major". "I hope you aren't going to follow in his footsteps, he used to go sick with an ulcerated toenail!" What a reference! From then on, whenever I came into contact with the Sergeant Major, his old moustache would twitch and I would have the feeling I was carrying the can for the old man!

In those days, my father was six feet two inches tall and weighed around sixteen stone. He was endowed with great physical strength and had arms like tree trunks. I've known him to lift considerable weights and he was extremely fit. When working on the farm he made light work of lifting sacks of corn which weighed eighteen stone. One day a farmer said to him, "What, can you lift a coomb of corn, Fred?" to which Father replied, "Yes, and you on top". This he proceeded to do, lifting the coomb of wheat which weighed eighteen stone and the farmer weighing sixteen stone on top!

When I was in the army, the old timers used to tell me of his strength. Apparently he once carried three troopers on his back. To do this he placed a wooden form on his shoulders, one trooper sat on it with his legs around Father's neck and the others each end. Like most country people, he had a very dry sense of humour and had the ability to notice characteristics in other people enabling him to mimic entertainingly.

After Father came out of the army, we seemed to have an addition to the family every year until finally there were eight of us. Times were hard and sometimes Father came home with only twelve shillings to keep all of us for a week. However, as he was the biggest poacher in the area, six of the family survived — five boys and one girl.

My earliest recollections are of walking the woods, meadows and fields with my father. One of my first lessons was how to move quietly and quickly, in daylight looking where you put your feet and at night testing the ground with the toes before putting your whole weight on the foot. I also learned how to glide amongst the bushes and trees and remain unobserved in the undergrowth. Next I learned how to shoot in the dark. I was taught how to observe a bird in a bush or tree, then how to detect a bird quickly, using the lights of the city on the horizon in order to see its silhouette.

As soon as I was old enough, I accompanied Father on his poaching expeditions, always on the darkest and wildest of nights with the rain falling hard or the wind howling. As our eyes became accustomed to the dark, I had to put into practice all I had been taught. When such a night presented itself, Father put on his poacher's jacket which had a big inside pocket. He would take his folding four-ten gun down from the rack and at the press of a button, the gun was folded and tucked away inside the pocket. The outside pockets were loaded with cartridges, the short four-ten on one side and on the other, the heavier and more powerful long four-ten. With the big old side-bag over his shoulders, we were away, slipping quietly out of the back door, across the fields, looking into the spinney, examining the hedgerows and looking at the thorn trees in the big straggly hedges. When we had finished the hedgerows and pit-holes, we carried on to the big wood. The

larch is one of the first trees in the season to attract poachers, being the first to shed its needles. If we knew of a young larch plantation, it was the first to be visited. When the night was really rough with gale force winds, the birds always favoured a pit-hole. These were man-made holes, former marl and clay diggings which had since grown over with thorn bushes and small trees that gave excellent cover for the birds on a rough night. Sitting low in the trees the pheasants provided an easy target. If there was water in the pit-hole the birds, amazingly, always seemed to sit on branches overhanging the water. As we never took a dog out at night, we didn't bother to shoot them.

We always used the short four-ten cartridge when shooting birds sitting low in larch or hedgerows and the long cartridge for the oaks and other large trees. We preferred the shorter cartridge, when possible, to keep noise down to a minimum. Father had a special sight on his gun for night shooting. It was made out of an old car inner tube, cut to the shape of a V or, as we called it, 'a pair of rabbit's ears'. He cut a hole in the bottom to insert the barrel of the four-ten. When taking aim in the dark, he lined the pheasant's head between the crotch of the 'rabbit's ears' and when his four-ten cracked, down came the bird which I retrieved and put in the bag.

Father never shot a bird out of season. Once the shooting season had finished, that was it regarding pheasants or game. Anyway it was an additional charge if you were caught. I wasn't taught the ABC like other children — I learned the 'game laws'. These I knew off by heart at a very early age and the knowledge came in very useful later on in life. The principal charges were:

Trespassing in pursuit of game;
Killing game out of season;
Being in possession of game;

17

Shooting game on a Sunday;
Killing game without a licence.

We called being charged with all five offences 'getting a nap hand'.

Our only income after the shooting season was from rabbits and hares, until the nesting season, when I was sent primrosing — which was a cover-up. All the banks on the hedgerows were covered with primroses which gave a good camouflage for my nesting expeditions. I had to find any pheasant eggs in the hedgerows and mark their position so that I could find the nests later. Very often I had 'keepers accost me, thinking I was bird-nesting, kick my backside and send me home. I had to relate to my father all my findings and my markings and when it was dark he found the nests that were not being sat on and took the eggs. He had a special trilby hat with a torch inside which pinpointed the markings, and subsequently the nests. Two villages away he had a contact who purchased all the eggs. The buyer then sold them to the estates for rearing there. Nowadays the eggs are placed in an aviary, but in those days, 'keepers used to buy extra eggs and put them under hens for rearing to help swell their stocks. Very often Father sold eggs which found their way back to the estates from which they had come in the first place!

We had two lurchers which swept up anything in their path, especially hares and rabbits. One was black and the other white. Something I could not understand at the time was that when we were out in the dark and we knelt down to see the silhouette of the dogs against the skyline and I would say to Father that I could see the white one and Father would reply that it was the black one. It took me a long time to puzzle it out, but in fact anything dark stands out clearly on the horizon, whereas a lighter object is obscure.

When we were preparing to net the rabbits, Father first sent me to the selected field in daylight — no one questions a small boy walking around a field near the hedge. I had to clear any debris that might foul the net. Then, when the weather and night were suitable, we would wear old coats without buttons, tied round the waist with string so that the net would not get snagged up in the dark. The net, which was about a hundred yards long, together with a bundle of stakes, was tucked under Father's arm as we set off in the dark. Father's friend Jack usually accompanied us on these occasions to give a helping hand.

When we arrived at the field, Father would run the net out, making sure the wind was in the right direction, that is, blowing from the rabbits towards the net. He then put the stakes in every four yards to secure the net, leaning the stakes towards the rabbits. There had to be plenty of slack in the net which then covered about eighty yards. The net had to be slack or the rabbits would have hit it at high speed and bounced off. Father and I walked quietly to the top of the field where we tied a length of string around our wrists, spaced ourselves a hundred yards apart and walked towards the net, the string between us trailing through the grass. You could hear the rabbits scurry off in the direction of the net where Jack was ready to grab them, break their necks and put them in the bag.

Netting for pheasants or partridges was much harder work. It took two strong men to pull the net successfully as the weight would be considerable. Jack and Father would be on each end, the net being thirty-two feet wide and sixteen feet deep and shaped like a letter V with a rope running through the loop at the top to keep it taut. They walked over the field holding the net at shoulder height and letting it tail out behind them. If we came across a covey of partridges, we dropped the net flat to cover them and usually got the whole covey that way. Our favourite crop was rye grass, the net gliding over this like silk. Hay bottoms and all undersown stubbles were suitable, the birds favouring these spots to jug down

at night. A clean stubble was not suitable as the net roared like a train over it; sugar beet was all right providing there were no seedy beet present to protrude and stop the net from flowing.

On Saturday afternoons and Sunday mornings we would get the ferrets, nets and dogs and go off rabbiting which was great fun. One day when we were going home, we heard a car coming — quite an event in the village in those days. It stopped near us and out stepped a police sergeant. He told us to turn our bags out to which Father replied, "I'm not turning that bag out, but if you want to, carry on". The sergeant promptly grabbed the bag thinking it was full of pheasants. He was absolutely flabbergasted when twelve rabbits fell to the floor and out jumped three live ferrets which then ran all over the place. Father said, "You turned them out, you pick them up". The poor man had never handled a ferret or even seen one by the look on his face. Father let him sweat for a little while before he sent me to retrieve them.

On this occasion we had permission to go rabbiting on the farm but some of our rabbiting expeditions were strictly illegal. Had we been caught, we would have been charged with trespassing in pursuit of coneys.

We always kept lurchers and Father was constantly doing deals with dogs. 'To see a man about a dog' was a familiar story in our house. They all had to prove their worth as working dogs or they were sold or given to a good home as a family pet. On the heath outside the village we released the dogs to hunt the rabbits. A bagful of rabbits could be caught in the early morning with a good dog.

One old dog of ours, called Blue, was a true Norfolk lurcher, a cross between an Old English sheepdog and a greyhound — with brains from the sheepdog and speed from the greyhound. If we took him for a walk and marked anything, we could always send him back later to retrieve it. He brought us many a dinner! One day I remember, Father looked out of the window and there had been quite a heavy fall of snow. He remarked, "What's that old dog doing lying in the snow, why isn't he in his kennel?" He pulled his boots on and went outside and when he looked in the kennel, it was obvious why the dog couldn't get in — it was full of hens! I think we lived on chicken for weeks after that episode. We never did hear who had lost any chickens, though Father kept his ear to the ground whenever he visited the pub!

Father did less well when he purchased another lurcher for the only thing that dog ever brought home was hedgehogs. Like Blue, this old dog was bought from some gypsies and was no doubt of great value to them, but we didn't eat hedgehogs!

Father had guns of all descriptions, including the folding four-ten and four-ten disguised as a walking-stick. On this, the silver band just below the handle twisted to allow the trigger to drop out of its slot, then by twisting the handle from left to right, the breach opened to insert the cartridge. Removal of the cork in the end made it ready to fire. He also possessed a twelve bore pin-fire which had a special cartridge with a pin protruding at the side, not with the cap in the centre as today. When the gun was fired, the hammer came down to strike the pin. These cartridges were very dangerous to handle.

I even remember an old muzzle-loader amongst Father's collection, which had a ram-rod clipped to the bottom of the barrel. To use the gun you had a shot flask, powder flask and a tin of caps. The powder flask was made of copper and the shot flask of leather. Both had a measure at the end to obtain the correct amount when loading. To load the gun, a measure of black powder was poured down the barrel, followed by a large sheet of newspaper rammed down with the ram-rod to form a wad, then a measure of shot with another sheet of newspaper rammed in. It was always kept loaded and if stood for any length of time, the explosion would be all the more powerful. When Father took it out, he would put the cap on the nib and let the hammer gently down onto the cap. Taking aim, he pulled the hammer back and squeezed the trigger. It went off like a cannon and the surrounding area would be strewn with shreds of the *News of the World* or *John Bull!* Then he had a few anxious moments to wait while the smoke cleared to see if he had killed his prey. An old muzzle-loader took some holding because of the recoil and Father wasn't too particular as to the amount of powder he used! For shot, anything available was put in, such as old cycle ball-bearings.

One day a man living three doors away came to the door and said, "Fred, there's a pigeon sitting on your chimney". Father thought this would be good opportunity to get the gun unloaded. It had been loaded for about a month and was well primed. He asked Billy if he would like to shoot it and handed him the gun. Billy tried to take aim but found the eaves of the roof were in the way. Father suggested he stand in the wheelbarrow which stood away from the house near the flower beds. So Billy climbed into the barrow, took aim, pulled the trigger and an almighty roar ensued. When the smoke and the paper had cleared, Billy was in the middle of the garden, the pigeon had gone and so had two chimney-pots!

We had a policeman in the village whose nickname was Samson, because of his great strength, I suppose. He knew of Father's escapades and would dearly have loved to nab him. Trying to be sociable one evening, he said to Father, "If you drop onto an old hare, Fred, I'm rather partial to one". So early the next Sunday morning, Father took the dog onto the heath, but catching a hare, he didn't kill it but took it gently away from the dog, put it in a sack and tied the top. He gave it to me and said, "Boy, take this down to the policeman and tell him this is a present from Fred. And tell him he's not going to have me for killing ground game on a Sunday!"

He was constantly brushing with the law. The village policeman and the gamekeepers were well aware of his poaching. When there had been a lot of poaching in the surrounding area, it was nothing for us children to wake up in the middle of the night and hear strange voices which meant the house was being searched. Nothing was ever brought home after an expedition, it was always planted along with the gun and retrieved later. I often saw Mother and Father go out walking on Sunday afternoons with the baby in the pram, one of those big boat-prams with a false bottom. When they reached the spot where Father had planted the game, they lifted the baby out and put the birds in the bottom, coming home with nobody the wiser.

There were several gamekeepers employed on the neighbouring estates and Father kept a constant vigil as to their whereabouts. Indeed, we were instructed as children to report anything and everything unusual. When coming home from work, if Father saw an old bird going up to perch, he would mark the spot and go back later.

Of course, Father had his customers. A pheasant in those days made half-a-crown and we couldn't afford to eat them unless one was shot up and no good for sale, then it went in the pot. I was sent on these expeditions after dark, Father giving me the shopping bag with a brace of birds inside and saying, "Take these down to old Joe's and tell him they were shot yesterday. The cost is five shillings".

I always had to go to the back door. Timidly knocking on the door, I had to wait in the dark, and when the door was answered, I recited my piece and held out my hand for the five shillings. Very often when I received the money I had to carry on to the shop, which was always open until late. Mother gave me a list which I handed over the counter with the five shillings. It took me all my time to carry home the bag which would be laden with provisions. You could buy two pounds of sugar for tuppence ha'penny and if things were good, I sometimes got a ha'penny to buy a gobstopper.

The butcher was always a good customer. I suppose he could buy from Father cheaper than anywhere else and I don't believe he had a game licence. I remember one time taking my bag and saying my piece. The butcher looked at the birds and said, "Tell your father I can only give you three shillings as the old cock has had his head blown off". I was flabbergasted and ran home to tell Dad the tragic news. I was sent back with the news, "Father wants the old cock back. He reckons he can't let it go for that money". I took the bird home in the bag to find Father had gone out on his bike. When he returned he said, "I've found where I downed the old bird and I've got the cock's head". He went straight to Mother's workbox and taking out needle and thread, said to Mother, "Come on gal, just sew this old cock's head on for me". When the deed was done, I had to return it to the butcher after being told to make sure I got the five shillings. The butcher examined the bird, muttered "God have mercy on the poor and needy" and gave me the five bob.

At one time Father worked for the miller delivering bags of corn by horse and cart to the various farms. These bags were coombs of corn, wheat weighing eighteen stone, barley sixteen stone and oats twelve stone. At one farm, the farmer said he wanted to show Father where he wanted the sacks stored. He walked into the barn and pointed upwards, "I want you to climb that ladder, walk along that plank to the landing, up the next ladder to the top landing and stack it there". Father took off his cap and scratching his head asked, "Would you mind telling me how you get your corn down from there?" "In stones and half-stones", replied the farmer. "Well, I suggest that is the way you take it up. Good day". Needless to say, he got the sack from that job!

He then went on a farm as a stockman. He enjoyed this job, preparing all the feed for the cattle and tending to their general well-being. The highlight of this job was on Saturdays when we were employed as drovers. This was a tiring day, driving cattle to market. The cattle market then situated in the centre of Norwich near the castle was always referred to as 'Norwich Hill' or 'up the hill', the task itself described as "bullock walloping up on the hill". We got up at three o'clock in the morning in all weathers, had breakfast and made our way to the farm to collect the cattle that had been selected the previous day for market.

Once on the road, I was directed to walk in front of the herd and Father walked at the rear. I had to make sure all the gates were shut on the way. If there was an opening without a gate, I had to stand at the entrance until the cattle had passed and then catch up at the front again. The going was all right along the country lanes, though very slow at the best of times, for we hardly saw a soul at that time in the morning. When we approached the outskirts of the city it was a different matter. I was constantly darting from one side of the road to the other to stop the cattle entering the numerous gateways. The traffic had to give way to us as we entered the city streets, all the shoppers making for the shop doorways for shelter as we drove past.

When we arrived at the Hill, Father had to find pens to put the cattle in. It was a rather precarious business but other drovers and farmworkers gave a hand. The job completed, we had a cup of tea and a cheese roll whilst waiting for the farmer to arrive. It was also interesting to look around and see all the different characters on the Hill. The professional drovers wore brown boots and buskins and a smock with a bright wrapper round the neck. They stood surveying all the cattle with their thumbs in their waistcoats — it was difficult to know if the cattle belonged to them or the farmer! Everyone seemed to know everyone else, the pubs were open until late in the afternoon and many a deal was struck over a pint of beer. Indeed a lot of dealers seemed to disappear into the pub and do a deal and then return to the sale for another one. It was certainly a very busy place, cars were still very rare at this time, so most farmers travelled by pony and trap. Leaving the sale ground, we had to start the long trek home, but Father always stopped at the first pub to have a couple of pints of beer, handing me a half-pint outside. This was my wages for the day for I never received any money from Father or the farmer. I know that half-pint tasted good and helped to fortify me for the rest of the long journey home.

One Saturday the farmer wanted us to take a load of sheep with the bullocks, which was a funny business as the sheep would go up one side and then the other. If they saw a hole in the hedge, they wandered through and if one went through, the rest were sure to follow. It was a dodgy job! Finally we got them to market but I think we walked twenty miles to travel seven!

The following Saturday there were only three calves to go to the Hill. We hitched the old cob to the flat-railed cart and loaded the calves in the back and covered them with a net. When we were going at a steady trot along the main road, one of the calves put his head under the seat and pushed it out of the pegs. This unloaded the pair of us — we went backwards into the cart with our feet up in the air! After we found our feet again, we soon put the seat back and finished our journey. It was a joy to ride there and home again despite the upset!

In the 1939–45 war, Father was in the Home Guard. As usual, the person in charge had no army experience — he was the village school master. One day he gathered the platoon around him and proceeded to demonstrate how to disarm the enemy by using the technique on Father. The school master made a grab for Father's rifle but Dad flicked his feet from under him and put the butt of the rifle to his throat, thereby demonstrating far more effectively the right method to use!

Father could work very hard. When he was hoeing sugar beet, he was up at daybreak, working until eleven o'clock or the heat of the day, returning about three o'clock and working until dusk. He always said, "You give a fair day's work for a fair day's pay. When people want more than you are prepared to give, it's time to move on, but never throw your dirty water out until you've got some clean!" He lived until he was ninety, so he didn't have a bad innings!

CHAPTER 2

Village Life

There were some very interesting characters in the village, people seem stereotyped today by comparison. Everybody had a nickname, goodness knows where they came from — Shymo, Shiddles, Lumber, Slippery, Scratch and Narbo to name but a few. As a child I never knew any of these people by any other name. I think some of them were handed down from one generation to another. In spite of the hard times people were happy and could get a laugh out of the simple things of life, if something or somebody was good for a laugh it went from house to house.

The meeting place was the blacksmith's shop. I suppose it was always warm in there, so if you wanted to know anything that was the place to call.

On one of my visits to the blacksmith's, Fred was bemoaning that he had a headache. Apparently the night before he had a jar too many and his head was a little sore. He said, "Of all the mornings, I have got to shoe the donkey from the Rectory." As the donkey was a bit low to the ground Fred didn't relish the job. I had seen this donkey in the village pulling a large basket on wheels which contained the laundry. Fred said, "You stand at the door and keep look out. I'll soon knock a set of shoes on him." He reached under the donkey and grabbed the off hind and off fore

legs and turned him onto his back. He then proceeded to straddle the donkey's body, sitting on the stomach with the donkey's feet up in the air. Operating in this position he gave him a new set of shoes in no time at all.

Also in the village we had a 'nosey parker'. People would lay bets that you wouldn't get past her door at any time of the night or day without her seeing you.

One old boy I remember suffered from depressions and was always threatening to take his life. People got so used to him that they didn't take any notice of his threats. One day when he was in a mind to make off with himself, he climbed into the apple tree at the bottom of his garden, tied a rope around a branch, then around his neck. He threw himself out of the tree to the ground. Fortunately, or unfortunately, he made the rope too long and walked around with a limp for weeks!

Charlie was the old chicken dealer. He had a pony and cart and lived in a cottage in the village and always had a load of chicken crates on the back of the cart. When he went into his cottage he took the bridle and harness off his pony and hung it on the stair-rail. He had a permanent 'dew drop' on the end of his nose and several days' growth on his chin, a big old coat and a wrapper around his neck. Every Saturday he harnessed up his old pony and cart and trotted off to Norwich Hill to do his deals. Everybody knew Charlie was a rogue and that you had to watch him carefully as he was out to do you. All the time he was doing a deal, he kept up a constant chit-chat to cover his crooked ways. For example, he bought up old hens, rubbed lipstick in their combs, descaled their legs with paraffin and they passed as point of lay pullets — until it rained!

Charlie once sold Mother some ducks, which he delivered with some eggs in the crates, saying "Here you are Ruby, they are full in lay". Mother kept them for weeks and didn't get any eggs.

Inspecting them one day she noticed they were shooting curly feathers on their tails — they had been drakes all the time and he had pulled the tail feathers out.

He was a great user of the pub and a singer of all the songs of long ago. His old pony took him home many a time. Once after a convivial lunchtime in the pub, he went home. Some hours later he realized he had lost his overcoat. Returning to the pub the landlady informed him that he had sold it earlier for five shillings!

Father's brother never did marry but lived with Grandmother. His name was Horace but we used to call him 'Hoddy'. He was six feet two inches tall, very thin and he always wore drain-pipe trousers with a matching country jacket. A thin white silk scarf was tied around his neck, the ends of which crossed over and under his braces and tied in front of his chest. On his head he wore a trilby with a rather large brim, on his feet size fourteen hob-nail boots. When I was a child I used to start at the floor and look up thinking I would never come to the end of him. Being single his pockets jingled and he could afford to be a good customer at the pub; I think this was his main hobby. He walked down to the pub around eight o'clock and by ten o'clock he would be well away. He used to sing a little song:

> I never knock at the wrong street door,
>   may I beg your pardon,
> When I go home I can always tell,
>   by the little tree growing in the garden.

This he sang in a very loud voice doing a little clog dance at the same time. The sparks literally flew as his hob-nail boots struck the pantiled floor.

My Grandmother, Hoddy's mother, was a rather particular old lady — very prim with her hair neatly pinned and she always wore a big white apron. There was a small table at the bottom of her stairs where she kept her pride and joy, an aspidistra, together with a candle-stick and box of matches for Hoddy to light his way to bed. One night Hoddy came home a little the worse for wear and looking for the little tree growing in the garden, he went to bed. In the morning when Hoddy put in an appearance with a bit of a thick head, Grandmother said, "Hoddy, where's my aspidistra?" "Oh dear," exclaimed Hoddy, "I didn't think it gave a lot of light last night!"

When Grandmother died, Hoddy went to live with a sister and when she died, rather than see him go into a home, Father took him in. Our house was bursting at the seams but it didn't matter; we all had to move up one and make room for Hoddy.

Once we were having a bit of trouble with stray cats getting in through the bedroom window from a roof immediately below. Early one morning Father called me and said, "Shut your window up, a cat has just crept in." We heard the cat go downstairs and both crept down after it. Seeing us, the cat just took off, raced around the room and jumped up the curtains, clawing them to ribbons in an effort to reach the top. Father grabbed the first thing handy, which was one of Hoddy's size fourteen boots, hurled it at the cat, missed, but knocked the window out. The cat immediately jumped through the hole and was gone.

Of course in the early days of my life, the village was very isolated. There was no public transport, just a carrier's cart. Farmers and the well-off had a pony and cart, cycles were few and far between and people walked for miles in all weathers to their place of work. The roads were very rough, just sand and stone rolled down with a steam roller. The lorries that came into the village to carry the sugar beet or corn were steam wagons or the old chain-driven lorries with solid tyres.

It was of great interest when a steam engine appeared in the village. I used to stand and watch them for hours. When they contracted to plough a field they had two steam engines, one at each end of the field pulling the plough across the field with a wire hawser. A man used to sit on the plough, operating a steering wheel to keep it straight in the furrows. When one engine finished pulling the plough, he gave a blast on the steam whistle for the engine on the other side to pull it back. This method was also used for sub-soiling with a gyrotiller, which was a large round implement which revolved deeply into the soil, churning it like a giant liquidiser and getting down deeper than a plough.

The men who worked the steam engines lived on the job, towing a shepherd's hut mounted on iron wheels, behind the steam engine. Inside were bunks, a cupboard to store their few possessions, and a tortoise stove with a chimney pipe. Most of the cooking appeared to be done on the steam engine. Father and I used to walk to the field to see Sam who was a driver. When he cooked a meal he rubbed a shovel over with a piece of rag, laid thick pieces of bacon on the shovel and inserted it in the furnace door. While the bacon sizzled a couple of eggs were added, and then eaten with chunk of bread from an old enamelled plate. I have seen him cook kippers in the same way. An old teapot was always in evidence with a tin of condensed milk. Sam could always come up with a yarn over a cup of his brew. For washing — which wasn't very often — he took water from the engine. A steam engine seemed to me a very useful thing to have as everything was at hand. Once they had all the gear set up they worked around the clock to complete a field. Then they damped the fire down to take a rest before moving on to another field.

Sam had an old bike hung on the back of the engine and when he had a break, he unhooked the cycle and came down to the village to shop or call at the pub for a pint. I remember he used to chew tobacco like a piece of rope, called a plug. After he had chewed it he put it in his waistcoat pocket and in the evening he dried it out in front of his fire and then smoked it in his pipe.

Of course, harvest time was the highlight of village life, harvest being a significant time. If a baby was due to be born it was reckoned to appear either before or after harvest. And with jobs, people said, "I'll leave that until after harvest."

As soon as the harvest started the village was a hive of activity, the men working from early in the morning until late at night. Father would contract with the farmer to do a harvest for eleven pounds. The alternative was to take it by the month at day rate plus overtime. Father chose the former for if the weather held good you could sometimes get it done in three weeks. Occasionally, if the farmer felt generous he would give you the oats at day work plus overtime rates because oats have to stand for a longer period as the straw is greener — 'the first cut and the last to cart.'

Usually it worked out one man to eleven acres of corn. The eleven pounds included all the jobs of cutting, shocking-up, carting, stacking and thatching, a colossal effort with long hours of sweat and hard work to get it done in time. The harvest moon very often put in an appearance before Father returned home.

He went prepared for a long day with his 'nines', lunch and 'fours' all packed in a frail basket, complete with several bottles of drink. This was mostly cold tea, brewed and poured into bottles with a little sugar added but no milk and this was very refreshing on a hot day. A bottle of ginger beer and a bottle of home made lemonade were also taken as he needed plenty of drink to replace the sweat, and wash the dust out of his throat during the hot sunny days.

It was the same with the horses, very long days and plenty of hard work. The farm boy was responsible for carting the feed bins onto the harvest field as well as the water tank for the horses' rest period. If three horses were used to a binder, it required twelve on the field at one time, two binders being worked. Each team would work for two hours. The water tank had to be topped up and stood in a shady spot so the horses could enjoy their rest period away from the flies which plagued them in hot weather.

The men started the field by cutting the headlands with a scythe; one man in front mowing, another following behind collecting the swarth and tying it into a sheaf. Several pairs worked at this stage, all swinging to a rhythm of the scythe, pausing now and again to sharpen the blade with a rub which he drew from his belt at the back.

Once when Father was doing this job the farmer remarked, "My word, Fred, your scythe takes a lot of sharpening," to which Father replied "I get as much for sharpening as I do for swinging!"

For mowing corn they had a length of hazel tied to the heel of the scythe and connected at the top of the handle, shaped to a bow. This was called a boil. At a sweep of the scythe the swarth hit the boil, placing it in a neat ridge ready for the man following to gather and tie with a bond. As the men cut the headlands to make way for the binder, they always cut the corners to reduce the corn to a round clump to enable the binder to work in a circle. Parts that were laid to ground level due to rough weather had to be cut by hand as the binder could not negotiate these laid patches.

Once the field was cut, all the sheaves had to be shocked, six to eight sheaves to a shock and then left to dry out before carting to the stackyard.

When a field was being harvested the message travelled around the village like wild-fire. "They're cutting the twenty acres" would be the cry. This induced all the children and those that were free to descend on the field with sticks and dogs after the rabbits. As the binders completed their final rounds reducing the corn to a small patch, the rabbits wildly ran for cover. These rabbits were bred in the corn and suddenly finding themselves in wide open spaces they were startled to such a degree that they became easy prey for the sticks and dogs. One hundred to one hundred and fifty rabbits out of a field was commonplace when it came to the final count. When they had completed the field, they were laid on the canvas of the binders and taken to the gateway where they were freely distributed amongst the farmworkers and anyone helping to catch them. A harvest rabbit was in good order and a very welcome gift. My mother made the most delicious rabbit pies, or baked them with pork slices.

Most of the boys were 'hold-gee' boys. This entailed collecting the sheaves off the shocks to take them to the stack. For this they had a horse and wagon, the boy shouted, "hold-gee" which was the signal for the men on the wagon to hold tight as he was moving to the next shock. I have done this job and received the sum of one pound for a harvest. This money was used to rig me out to go back to school You could buy a pair of boots for five shillings, knee-length socks, trousers and a pullover accounted for the rest of the money.

When the fields were cleared, again the message went around the village, for wives and children to go gleaning. We always kept chickens in the backyard, so this was very handy to pick up the ears of corn that had been missed to help keep the fowls throughout the winter.

The dust and muck were terrific, especially on a still day, and we always liked a breeze to blow it away. As the stack diminished in size, the rats and mice gradually worked their way to the stack bottom, which was made of hedge trimmings and bracken. When the men cleared all the sheaves they turned the stack bottom over to expose the rats and mice to the waiting terriers, which had a heyday. Dogs in the village only needed to hear the drum start up and they invited themselves along for the day. When threshing was finished, there was a heap of muck which came out of the drum, which contained all the weed seeds. When the tackle moved

away the birds moved in. We do not see quantities of birds like those today; there were sparrows, linnets, goldfinches, greenfinches and yellow hammers, all in great numbers.

Another thing we never see today are the insects. I remember when I was a 'hold-gee' boy taking the wagon to the stack and when it was unloaded the bottom was covered up to three inches deep with insects, ladybirds, earwigs etc. When I see disease in the trees today, I think of those days and wonder if modern farming methods have unbalanced the ecology of the countryside.

When the harvest was completed, all the men who had been employed for this task went to 'bush the stubbles'. This involved cutting blackthorn, loading it onto carts and distributing it over the stubbles, seven bushes to the acre. A bush was a branch of blackthorn about eighteen inches high, and when a site was selected a hole was made with a bushing iron and and the bush was inserted in the hole in order to anchor it against any high winds. All this was intended to deter would-be poachers with their long nets. The men usually doing this job on a Saturday morning, were paid by the head keeper.

Farming has changed over the years. In the old days, corn was cut very low by a binder as the straw was a precious commodity, and with no pesticides there were always plenty of weeds in the bottom of the stubble. Netting wouldn't work on the stubbles of today as being clean, they do not attract the game.

When all the chores were completed it was usual to spend a pound. My father's usually went in rigging out the lot of us for the winter for we all needed new boots and warm clothes. Maybe he had a pint or two out of it as well!

There was nowhere in the village for people to meet up, apart from the church, chapel or pub, the village pump or the blacksmith's shop. In summer the village green sometimes attracted a few religious speakers or at election time, there was a gathering, but on the whole, people kept to their own hearths.

It was a marvellous breakthrough when the first wireless set arrived in the village. I can well remember going to hear the Cup Final on the wireless. All the village boys, eager to hear, gathered with the farm workers, puffing away at their pipes, in a tiny cottage room thick with smoke!

Later on in winter when we threshed the stacks it was a very busy time. The steam engine arrived the night before, setting the drum beside the stack ready for an early start the next morning. All the coal had to be carted for fuel and the water cart was pulled alongside for topping up the boiler. Once the engine was started, it was left alight through the week, but damped down at night. On arrival in the morning the driver got up steam and secured the belt from the engine to the drum, taking great care to get the correct tension. When all was running smoothly, work commenced. The pitcher on the stack lifted the sheaves with his two-tyne fork, pitching them to the man who worked on the threshing drum. They had to be presented ears first to this man, who was the bond cutter. He had a sharp knife with a serrated edge, strapped to his wrist to prevent it dropping into the drum. When cutting the bond around the sheaf he discarded the string, opened the sheaf up and gently fed it into the beaters of the drum. The beaters separated the corn from the ears which were dropped onto a sieve where the corn was separated from the chaff. A blower on the drum blew the light husk off the sieve into a chute, from where it was bagged up and used for cattle feed. The corn was shaken on the sieve to separate the 'dross' from the good corn, and continued on to individual chutes where it was bagged. The straw was cleared away from the drum by an elevator and made into a straw stack.

When it came to building the stacks, one man was the stacker responsible for the building and he was helped by two others, one pitching from the elevator, the other binding behind the stacker.

The stacks looked very stately in the stackyard. Great pride was taken in their building and the handywork including the thatching, stacking and the corn dollies which adorned the gable ends was admired by other farm workers. Sometimes a stack developed a lean if enough care hadn't been taken in the building, then it had to have a prop, or 'leg' as we called them, to hold it up. The builder had to take a ribbing if this happened, with remarks like, "If you put any more legs on that stack it will walk out of the stackyard!"

In the village we had a butcher, though not as we understand a butcher to be today. He didn't have a shop, just an outbuilding and a yard where the men used to slaughter the cattle, all in full view of the road. I used to stop and watch on my way to school, my curiosity being aroused by the squealing and bellowing that went on. The beasts had a rope put around their necks and were dragged to a block and pole-axed in the centre of the head, not killed by the humane methods we use today. The meat was hung in the outbuilding and then cut into joints and taken around the village by horse and cart. In the back of the cart were enamel dishes and trays with all the meat displayed in the various joints. The cart was covered in with doors at the back and was painted white inside. As it called from house to house, customers came out with their plates to make their purchases.

We had what was called a bake office where bread was made but a lot of people used to bake their own bread. It wasn't a proper shop though you could buy at the back door. The bread was taken around the village stacked on the back of a cart and covered with heavy flour sacks to keep out the rain or the dust. We took cakes to the bakery to have them baked. Mother would make a cake, which we called 'rough cut,' it was put in a large tin and the baker charged one penny to put it in the oven when he had finished bread baking.

A travelling cart called once a week delivering paraffin for lamps, hardware, cleaning and dry goods.

People were very superstitious in those days, my own mother continually coming out with the old sayings which all had a meaning. Mother never turned a gypsy away from the door without buying or giving them something for if you didn't encourage them they might put a curse on you. Whenever they came on their tours of the village, she would always have her hand read and never recounted the predictions in case they didn't come true. Dreams too were considered very important. The interpretation of some of these had great significance, usually tragic, bringing a foreboding outlook on which to ponder. Any symbol of good luck was readily accepted to brighten her future.

The children in the village played all the typical childhood games, in their seasons, whip and spinning tops in the spring, marbles in summer, hoops in winter to keep warm by bowling them along with a stick. Now and again boredom would set in as with all children. A great source of revenue and entertainment was Mr. Polton the old shoemaker. He lived in a cottage tucked away from the centre of the village. Mr. Polton's means of transport was a donkey and cart. Ned the donkey was left tethered to a stake on the village green, the stake being moved each day to give him fresh pasture. One of the tricks was to pull up the stake then run to Mr. Polton's shed and tell him the donkey had broken loose. He immediately got very agitated because catching the donkey was beyond his physical capabilities. He used to say, "Catch him for me and I will give you a penny." The children would hasten back to the green, re-stake the donkey and then return for the penny. The shop was the next to be visited to get a penny's worth of gobstoppers and have a share out. I often wonder if Mr. Polton knew of the tricks which we played, but these little escapades were great fun, the children creating their own amusement. They all helped to entertain our not very eventful lives.

My uncle Geoff, when he was a boy, used to have a goat with a proper leather harness to couple him to a small cart. Geoff used this transport to fetch the milk from the farm and to carry out Grandmother's errands. He would virtually have to pull the goat out of the village, but on the return journey the goat went like the clappers and Geoff very often had to hang on for dear life when coming down Stocks Hill.

I can remember Father visiting a neighbour who had a rather sick dog. I went along with him, being full of curiosity. Father said to Tom, "That dog's got worms," to which Tom replied, "Do you reckon?" "Yes," said Father. "I will give him some de-worming powder." Unable to contain myself for I didn't think Father had made the right diagnosis — I exclaimed, "I thought only furniture had worms!"

CHAPTER 3

My Childhood

Even though Father subsidized the house-keeping with his poaching we were extremely poor and I can't remember a time when I wasn't hungry. We had good parents who always did the best they could for us but unfortunately, being a growing lad, there was always a rat gnawing in my stomach!

We had a huge table in the centre of the living room which seemed to take up the entire room. It had a white wood top that was constantly scrubbed and used for everything including ironing, baking and meals. The 'baby' sat next to mother at meal-times and as each new one became old enough to sit at table we all moved round one. As I was the eldest, it wasn't long before I was sitting next to Father — then I had to watch my step! There was strong discipline in the house, we were not allowed to talk during meals apart from 'please' and 'thank-you', and we had to present ourselves clean. This meant dipping a bowl in the soft water butt outside and having a cold wash — even on the coldest of days we had to strip off and have a good wash.

Saturday night was bath night. A 'copper' was heated by fire wood and the galvanized bath brought in. The performance started at four o'clock with a hair cut, a flea-comb through the hair, then the bath and hair wash with carbolic soap. Afterwards we had tea which was, more often than not, bread and dripping, then the

highlight of the week — a toffee — before bed.

Christmas dinner was a brace of poached pheasants, a brace of rabbits and plenty of home-grown vegetables with egg pudding which was similar to Yorkshire pudding but of a spongier consistency. We had this for starters with gravy, followed by meat and vegetables, then Christmas pudding and custard. The custard was made with eggs and had two laurel leaves put in the milk before it was brought to the boil. This custard was lovely and creamy and had an almond taste from the laurel leaves. My mother always used this custard for trifles, etc. We had home-made ginger wine and ginger beer, and for presents, one small toy and a stocking containing sweets, nuts and an orange.

Boxing Day was the only time I can remember going out as a family, when we walked three miles to the next village to visit Grandmother. Such was the family that Grandmother had children much the same age as us, my mother being the eldest of her children. We had a get-together in her small cottage which was a smallholding situated way down a loke on its own. Grandmother spread large raisins on a meat dish, sprinkled them with brandy and set a match to them. They immediately burst into a blue flame and while they were burning you had to grab them and pop them in your mouth. This was called playing 'snapdragons' and was great fun.

However, a not so happy event which is embedded in my memory is the eviction from our cottage. I was ten years old at the time and the eldest of six. Apparently Father had a disagreement with the farmer for whom he worked. It all came about with the sugar beet crop being exceptionally good and with such a large yield it was difficult to earn much money, the rate being thirty shillings an acre to pull, top and knock. The farm men decided amongst themselves they would be better off doing the sugar beet at day work rates. The farmer approached Father as he lived in the tied cottage on the farm, to see if he would lead the men when working day work rates. This entailed setting the pace and keeping the men on the go. Father was adamant when he said, "They are all my mates and we all work together. No, I will not lead them." The farmer was furious at Father's decision and told him to either do the job or get out of our cottage. Father was forced, by loyalty to his workmates, to do the latter.

It was a very worrying time for my parents and we children soon sensed something was horribly wrong. Father eventually got another job but no house was available so he was served notice of eviction and notified of the date on which the bailiff was to take action. Having no money and nowhere to go with six children must have been a headache. For days he tried to find somewhere for us and time was running out. Fortunately the day before we were due to be evicted, he came home with the good news that he had found temporary accommodation some four miles away. It was a large farmhouse owned by two sisters who had considered father's plight and decided to let half of the farmhouse to him on a temporary basis.

Mother and Father were overjoyed at the news, as it was a load off their minds but they didn't tell a soul! The cottage we lived in was situated in a dip with steps leading from the road down to the cottage, a drop of some twelve feet below road level. The bailiff and the policeman arrived at the appointed time and said they had come to carry out their duty and evict us. Mother and Father said, "Carry on!" They didn't make any attempt to pack anything but gladly left it all to the bailiffs to pack all the crocks, the linen and bedding and cart it up the steps onto the road. The policeman was very upset and said, "I'm not very proud of my uniform today, Fred." He had to help carry all the furniture and effects. As children we found it difficult to understand what was going to happen to us all. When everything had been carried up the steps, Father went to collect a horse and wagon he had borrowed. We all loaded it up and climbing aboard, made our way to Old Maid's Farm, very grateful that we had somewhere to go and that our effects had all been carried up the steep steps for us!

These were supposed to be the 'good old days'. My sisters and brothers were very small at the time but this event was to be imprinted on their minds as a terrible experience. The farmhouse seemed very large compared with our small cottage. It had its advantages when playing hide-and-seek, and I can well remember playing skittles with my brothers and sisters in the long passages. The sisters who owned it were very good to us for the three months we lived there; then the Council found us accommodation and we moved back to the village.

Although there was no pocket money in those days, I always had my chores to do — sticks had to be got in, water carted from the well and logs and coal brought in before going to school, for all the cooking was done in a wall-oven and over an open fire. After doing my chores I was off to the heath with the dogs to give them a run before school. Very often in school I nodded off, for I had done a morning's work before I got there, and had sometimes been up late the previous night helping Father with the poaching. My mind wasn't on school anyway — it was usually up on the heath with the wild life.

When I look back to my own children and remember them plaguing me for a bed-time story, I stop and reflect that nobody ever read to me. They didn't have the time. Life was all about survival — culture didn't come into the curriculum at home or at school, just the 'three R's' and that was it.

We had three classrooms in the school, one each for infants, juniors and senior children. I think we must have been an unruly lot although discipline was very strict — the cane was always in use for the slightest misdemeanour. One particular thing sticks in my memory. Once when the schoolmaster was explaining about the universe, he said, "The moon is 240,000 miles away from the earth. It is predicted that one day somebody will travel to the moon but you don't have to worry because it will never happen in your lifetime." Well, I have lived to prove him wrong!

If Mother was ever ill, or when she had a baby, I had to stay at home because we couldn't afford to have anybody in and Father had to work. Mother had her bed downstairs and instructed me how to prepare the vegetables and cook the dinner. I would have to lay the table, keep the fire going and run all the errands. When I look back I think I was more often at home than at school, the result being that I am to this day an excellent cook but not much of a scholar!

When I left school my knee-length trousers were discarded and I had my first pair of long trousers. I was fourteen years old and felt very grown up. My first work on leaving school was a day's threshing on a farm near the village. I worked on the straw-stack, pitching straw from the elevator to the stacker. The farmer said when he paid me, "Here you are boy, you have worked like a man, I will pay you like a man." He paid me the sum of six shillings which was a man's pay for a day. I felt worn out but elated to earn so much money in one day, even though it all had to go home to Mother.

Before a place could be found for me on the farm I had to go for a few weeks to help the old shepherd near the village. My duties were setting folds with hurdles, then cutting up the mangolds, swedes and turnips for the lambs. To do this I had a knife shaped like a hot-cross bun, and cut them all into small pieces. The old ewes needed watching for when I was busily working away, suddenly one of them would knock me up the backside and send me flying! For this job I received ten shillings and sixpence per week. I gave Mother the ten shillings and I kept the sixpence. I stayed with the shepherd until after the lambing season when I got a regular job with a tenant farmer on the nearby estate. Everybody had a nickname there — they called me 'Don-o!' About twenty men were employed on the farm and twenty horses.

I was the farm boy and cycled to the farm, arriving at seven o'clock in the morning, put my cycle in the shed and walked on through to the stable. When I walked through the door the hurricane lamp was casting a dim glow over the surrounding stalls. There was a strong smell of horses, ammonia and the old head team-man's tobacco. In the dim light of the stable he sat on the corn-bin waiting for the rest of us. He had to put in one hour before the farm men arrived to give the horses their breakfast, brush them down and get them ready for the day. If it was a very wet day and there was plenty of mud about he had all their tails braided and tied in a little pom-pom which made it easier for cleaning when they came in at night. Then in came the steward to give the orders: "You can go to plough, you can go harrowing, you can go rolling." Whatever you were working on, you yoked your horses according to the implements they were pulling. When all was ready we went out of the stable and waited in the yard for the head team-man to appear. He would approach the mounting block, get astride his horse and lead us out of the farmyard. We all followed until we branched off into the different fields. It was the same procedure at night: wherever you were working, you didn't leave your field until the head team-man went past, then you could follow.

Arriving back at the stable you unyoked your horse and the team-man took over again. While the horses were feeding, he would be brushing them down, after which they were turned out into the yard which was littered with fresh wheat straw. There was a lodge on each side of the yard if they wanted shelter, and a rack full of hay and a water tank. If after inspection, there was a horse which had lost a shoe, I had to take it up to the blacksmith the next

morning.

We had two head team-men and second team-men, each man responsible for the horses in his care. They were more or less vets in their own right, having a big medicine cabinet containing various bottles, liniment for strains, ointments for sore shoulders, drinks for colic. They tended all the horses' ailments. To work a horse well you had to feed it well, and these horses really had a well balanced diet. Each team-man had his own corn bin, which was under lock and key, from which he measured the feed for the horses according to the work they had been doing.

At times the head team-man had to go into Norwich. When this was necessary he had instructions the night before to allow time to get everything prepared. He took all the brass home to clean, arrived at the stable very early in the morning to clean the harness, braided the horses' manes and tails, putting coloured ribbons in, and polished their hooves with oil. Two horses pulled the wagon and they looked magnificent when they were turned out, the brass and leather shining and the martingale adorned with the old horse brasses. The horses knew they looked good and were going somewhere special and they held their heads high, ears pricked, and picked their feet up, looking vigilant. After all, these horses were used to working in the fields, they knew every gateway and hedgerow. It was like going on holiday for them to have a change of scenery.

On visits to the city they called at the Brewery to collect a load of 'drains,' which was the residue after the malt barley had been processed and it was used as feed for the cows. Sometimes they had the horrible job of carting fish offal from the herring industry. This came into Norwich railway station by goods train and had to be shovelled out of the wagons by hand, loaded up and brought back to the farm and stored on a muck-heap. Didn't it stink! In the spring time it was carted onto the fields and used for manure.

On the wagons they used a skid, which was a narrow metal tray about two feet long and six inches wide with a six inch upstanding edge. Before coming down a steep hill with a load on, the team-man stopped at the top of the hill and placed the skids in front of each back wheel. He then drew the horses forward for the wheel to be inserted in the skid. As he carried on down the hill the front wheels of the wagon rotated and the skids sleighed down the hill to prevent the cart bearing down on the horses and getting out of control. When he got to the bottom of the hill he backed the horses and retrieved the skids.

After the wagons were unloaded at the end of the day, the horses took them back to the cart shed. They knew this was the last journey of the day and as we backed the cart in, the horses would go backwards more quickly than they had gone forwards all day! It was a good job we had a bumper in the back of the cart shed which was made of wood and let into the ground about three feet from the wall. As the horse backed the cart the wheels hit the stop — without this they would have knocked the back of the cart shed out!

This farm had its own threshing tackle and steam engine, besides a mill. There was a variety of work and the land was very light and full of fowl grass (twitch). One of my first jobs was lifting the drag, which was a triangular wooden frame with two handles at the back and iron spikes distributed at intervals similar to a harrow. The fowl grass had to be freed from the spikes and to do this I had to tilt the whole thing. It was a job suitable only for a strong boy. The drag was pulled by three horses. After getting the grass to the top, we went over it with a set of harrows, then with the flat roll and finally a set of chain harrows. The twitch would all wind into balls whereupon we shook it out and burned it.

I spent most of my time horse-hoeing, day in and day out, mangolds, swedes, turnips and sugar beet. I led the horse but the only conversation I had all day with the operator was "to you" and "hold off." I loved working with horses and the men on the farm were a good crew to work with.

I remember one old boy, whose nickname was 'Scent'. He used to be the odd-job man, feeding the calves and cutting the hay and chaff. One day he was in the barn operating the engine to prepare the food when it back-fired. Sparks flew forty feet up into the air, into the thatched roof and started a fire. Poor 'Scent' panicked and ran to the water tank with a couple of buckets yelling, "Fire, fire, I'll give a thousand pounds to anybody who can put the fire out!" He ran back to the barn with his buckets full of water, set one down, threw the other in the direction of the roof. It went up about six feet and came down on top of him. He did the same with the next one but fortunately his cries were heard, resulting in the fire engine being called. They saved the barn but the roof was badly damaged.

In the evenings and at weekends I used to meet up with the other lads in the village. We all met on the bridge because there was no village hall in those days, and we were not old enough to use the pub. One of the older boys got permission from a farmer to use his barn so we could all meet there. We brought about a dozen candles and put them around the wall. Then out came the boxing gloves and we really got stuck into one another.

Apart from this we just messed about in the village. If any strange boys came onto our patch we used to say, "Out of town before sundown or under the pump you go." We had a large pump in the centre of the village and if we caught them we held them under it and gave them a soaking.

In the winter months I was often engaged in poaching with Father. After the shooting season we went out for rabbits. One summer morning we got up early to hear a boxing match on the radio and when it was over, Father said, "It's a good morning for getting a few rabbits." So off we went with the dogs and bag. We had a bagful of rabbits in no time and as we approached the road, I said, "Listen, I can hear a three speed on a bike." We both jumped to the same conclusion that it was the 'keeper out on his early morning rounds and immediately planted all the gear and walked to the gate. Leaning on the gate as the 'keeper approached, Father said, "Morning John." John was startled, but immediately stopped and swung round on his old bike and said, "What are you on? I'm going to search you." Father said, "You can search us, we are only taking the dogs for a stroll, and have you got a light?" He put a cigarette to his lips and John gave him a light and also the benefit of the doubt. We parted company and on our way home we doubled back and picked up the bag.

In the evening I met the 'keeper and got into conversation with him. He said, "You're keen on shooting aren't you?" I replied, "Yes, I like a shot." "Well, come and see me tomorrow night and we'll have a little walk round." I went as promised and found John on the rearing field, inside the hut. I think he was glad to have somebody to talk to, it being very quiet and lonely. There were three full-time 'keepers on the estate, who worked a rota system on the rearing field so that it was never left unattended, taking turns to sleep in the shepherd's hut. The 'keeper on the night shift took over at six in the evening. It was his job to provide the feed for the 'keepers for the next day. The rearing field was a hay field which was cut with the grass cutter into rides. This was to protect the birds from winged vermin. If the latter put in an appearance the chicks could run into the tall grass for cover. A hen in a coop had about eighteen chicks which ran on free range. The coops were situated on the rides about ten yards apart, well-spaced to prevent one hen clucking more loudly than another and drawing all the chicks.

John asked me if I would give him a hand to shoot some rabbits and I readily agreed. We walked the meadows and soon had a dozen rabbits. Back on the rearing field we quickly had a fire going. We skinned the rabbits and cut them up, putting them into a big old iron boiler over the fire. In another boiler we put dozens of cheap New Zealand eggs, which we boiled and left to cool. When the rabbits were cooked the meat was all pulled from the bones and put through a big mincer, together with the eggs complete with shells. On completion it was all mixed with biscuit meal and became the feed for the next day.

Each evening I helped John with this task and gave a hand to move the coops onto fresh ground. As soon as I finished work in the evenings and on Saturdays and Sundays, I was with the 'keepers. I enjoyed yarning to them and listened intently to all their talk about the wildlife.

The birds had to be shut up at night, a board being placed in front of the coop at dusk and removed at first light in the morning. Once a week while the pheasants were in the coop we dusted them with gape powder, which we blew in with bellows, to dislodge the gape worms which congregated in the birds' throats. After a month on the rabbit diet we used to steep wheat, boil it until it was soft and then pour it into a hessian bag to drain. The chicks were gradually weaned onto this to prepare them eventually for a corn diet.

When the birds were six weeks old they were carted into the woods. The coop had no bottom and at night, when the hen and chicks were shut in, the coop was gradually drawn onto hessian. Then, rolling the ends to get a firm grip to keep it taut, the coops were lifted onto the cart and the horse took them to the various woods. Our nights and days on the rearing field were then finished — we had some memorable times, brewing cups of tea around the fire after all the chores were done on the lovely summer evenings.

Come the shooting season, as I worked for a tenant farmer on the same estate, I took days off to go brushing and to help the 'keepers, which I thoroughly enjoyed. I was paid six shillings a day and shared a barrel of beer which was sent up at lunch time by the game cart. I watched points on shooting days to see how the pheasants were driven to give a good show, the placing of the guns and the value of a good gun dog. All my spare time was taken up with the 'keepers and I soon began to realize that there was another side to the game business (other than poaching) and that I was being converted to *the other side of the fence!*

CHAPTER 4

Army Life
and Rehabilitation

When I reached the age of eighteen, soon after the outbreak of World War II, I went to the recruitment office to join the Guards. I had to have three references and a medical. I obtained my references from the schoolmaster, the parson and the local doctor who all vouched for my good character. I presented these, filled in several forms and was given a medical which I passed as A1. Having collated all these documents, the recruiting sergeant turned down my application because I was under age. Astonished I said, "My friend joined the regiment a few weeks back and he was the same age as myself. How come he was old enough and I'm not?" The answer came back, "Well he caught the boat and you've missed it." Returning home very disappointed, I related my experiences to Father who said, "Well you know what the trouble is, boy, he put his age on one year and you must do the same. I should go back tomorrow." The next day I returned to the recruiting centre again where I went through the same procedures as the day before, the only difference being that I was one year older! When I told him my age, a sly grin crossed his face and he said, "You have been accepted, when would you like to join the regiment?" I replied, "Straight away." He informed me that there would be a short delay before I was posted so I went home to await my calling up papers.

When these duly arrived with my railway warrant and enlistment papers, I had to report to Cumbermere Barracks, Windsor, on the following Thursday. At the time, several young people were leaving the village to go into the Forces so I was only one of many. I had to get to Norwich and find Thorpe Station — I had never been on a train! When I arrived at Liverpool Street Station I found the Tube and made my way to Paddington Station where I caught the train to Windsor. This was all a bit bewildering to me as I had never been out of Norfolk before. I felt very strange indeed and very much the raw recruit when I eventually arrived at Cumbermere Barracks. I entered the portals of the barracks with several other recruits, all destined for the same treatment. The next day we all had another medical examination before being told that the regiment was at full strength and the army could not be responsible for us, therefore we had to pick up our railway warrants and return home until they notified us.

In the two days that I was at the barracks I had a chance to look around and to begin to see what I had let myself in for. I can remember looking down onto the square where the troopers were at drill and being very impressed by their smartness and their ability to operate in unison. Very aware of being a country boy, I told myself that I would never be able to do that. It was the understatement of a lifetime!

After a few days they sent for me yet again and from then on, after entering the regiment, I can truthfully say I never stopped running for a year, getting up early to feed and muck out the horses, having breakfast, reporting to riding school, cleaning tack. I was schooled, brainwashed and amongst all the others, made into a lean, fit soldier, and I was still hungry!

As I settled down and began to get used to army life, I soon realized that I had to stand on my own two feet and look after myself. Any spare time I had was spent in the gym. My Corporal of Horse, Jim, was sparring partner — before the War — to Len Harvey and Tommy Farr. He was a good tutor and at six feet three inches tall and weighing fourteen stone six pounds, he really put me through it. I thoroughly enjoyed boxing. I was also in the tug o' war team which was good fun when we put on displays in competition with other regiments.

The riding school I found very exacting. Working with horses on the farm was a far cry from being schooled with these horses. I often finished my round hanging onto the horse's neck, with remarks from the instructor, "Trooper, you do love your horse!" I had the same commands yelled at me every day, "Keep your head up, keep your heart up, keep your hands down, keep your heels down." One day when I had a particularly good horse I thought I had accomplished the course in style. The course comprised six jumps over the grid, pole, elm tree, wall, which was a solid brick wall, water jump and fence, table and lastly the in-and-out round two telegraph poles. I felt chuffed to think I had survived the round without any mishaps when the instructor came alongside me and said, "I suppose you are pleased with yourself. Next time you want to buy a bus ticket, after all you are only a bloody passenger!"

Eventually I became an experienced rider and when we got up early in the mornings and took the horses for exercise in Windsor Great Park, I was in my element. I found I was remembering all my father had told me and realized he was right in talking me into this regiment. I passed out as a Cavalryman twelve months later, thus qualifying for one week's leave. It was a very different person that returned to the village than the one that had left. Everybody made a great fuss of me and I had a good leave. When I returned I was posted to Knightsbridge Barracks in London.

When we arrived at Knightsbridge, the Blitz was in full swing and they were having trouble with the horses during air-raids. At

this time when the horses were in their stalls in the stable, they wore a neck strap which was chained to the manger. When the bombs started falling or the guns opened up in Hyde Park, there was a fear that the horses would endanger themselves when rearing up. Orders were given that every trooper must tend his own horse in the stable during raids and must try to hold the horse down and it was decided that the chains be taken from the manger. I used to get in the hay rack above the horse's head and when the horse reared, I tapped him on the head and said, "Down!" This seemed to work very well until one night I didn't bother with the hay rack, thinking the raid would be slight. When the gunfire started my horse reared, and when he came down, hit me on top of the head and a glancing blow on the shoulder. I couldn't get away from him — he had me penned up tight against the wall of the stall. When another explosion occurred, he swung round in the stall and kicked me into the gangway in the centre of the stable. The horse on the other side lashed out with his back feet and kicked me in the middle of the back, sending me flying into my own horse's stall. My horse by this time was running loose, and I was being trampled. They discovered me after the raid, unconscious and in a mess. I was taken to hospital where I remained for a few weeks.

When I returned to the barracks, it had been decided to take the horses to Windsor, from where they were to be taken to Melton Mowbray to be turned out to grass for the duration of the War. We then became mechanised, with scout cars, armoured cars and motor cycle combinations. The entire Battalion had to start training again as the reconnaissance unit for the Guards' Armoured Division. I did my training and became the driver of an armoured car, all the time being troubled by my right leg as a result of my accident. We moved to Bulford Camp on Salisbury Plain and then onto Trowbridge in Wiltshire. I kept complaining of pain in my lower back and right leg, so was referred to the Medical Officer but he couldn't find anything wrong with them. In fact I went back several times and began to get the feeling that they thought I was malingering. However one morning I couldn't get out of bed at all. I panicked as I had no control over my right leg whatsoever. The order was given, "Get this man to hospital," and I was taken to St. Martin's Hospital, Bath. I stayed there for two years having lumbar punctures, gold injections in the spine and electrical treatment but with little improvement. Life became very tedious at times, the War was at its height and I felt very lonely as none of the family could visit me. Apart from letters from Mother, my time was spent amongst the other patients playing cards and teasing the nurses. The Salvation Army came to sing carols at Christmas accompanied by their portable harmonium and they still found me there when they came the next year.

Eventually I was moved to a Military Hospital at St. Hugh's College, Oxford, for a further six months where the decision was made that nothing more could be done for me. The doctors said I would not walk again without the aid of crutches. Finally I was discharged with a full pension in May 1943. The pension was thirty shillings per week for a single man.

I had a train ticket to Norwich, a demob suit about two sizes too small, a pair of crutches and I had to make my own way home. Arriving at Norwich station, there were no taxis available. I waited around and managed to get a lift with the Royal Mail van to within one and half miles from home, which I had to walk on crutches. So much for army life!

At first it was great to be home with the family again, who had all grown up since my last leave. After I had caught up with all the news, it took a day or two to settle down. All the family were out of the house during the day and time soon began to drag as there was nothing much I could do except help Mother with a few chores. Although my leg was very troublesome, I felt all right in

myself, but so helpless. My mother was very organised in her household duties, she was always up early and worked at a great pace throughout the day, being used to caring for a large family. One day she was getting rather worked up because the fire wouldn't draw properly. Being wartime it was impossible to get the services of a chimney sweep. The chimney in question had always been a source of trouble as the chimney breast went off at a very acute angle, causing soot to congest in the elbow. I thought I would be helpful and help her out of a muddle. I went into the shed and found a box of black powder left over from my father's poaching days when he loaded the old muzzle loader. I wrapped a small amount of the powder in brown paper and made a small parcel, then soaked a length of string in paraffin which I tied around the packet, leaving a length for a fuse. I put this packet in the bend of the chimney with the aid of a bamboo pole. Opening the doors and windows I then placed a sheet over the fireplace, inserted my hand at the side and lit the fuse. While all this was going on, Mother waited outside, rather nervous of the outcome. There was a terrific roar and the next door neighbour came running out shouting, "Where did it drop Ruby?" thinking a bomb had dropped nearby. The chimney never troubled us again but the mess we had to clear up kept us busy for a day or two. The sheet I had put over the fireplace had blown away and there was soot everywhere. After this I think Mother was glad to get me out of the house whenever possible!

One day I had the idea of getting the old bike out. I made a stirrup on one pedal to insert my foot, which was a great success, and with a little practice I was away. It was great to get going under my own power until I came to a hill and had to walk. I limped along, somehow holding onto the bike. Gradually I got stronger and could control my leg for greater distances. I began taking the dog and the gun on the heath, cycling there and walking about to get a shot at a rabbit. Every now and again my leg let me down and I fell flat on my face. However, there was no-one to see me so I gathered myself up and carried on. It was wonderful to be out of the house and in the fresh air. The nerves in my leg were beginning to mend and after a year, when I went for my first medical since being discharged, I could walk quite strongly. I put this down to the therapeutic combination of fresh air and plenty of exercise and after the depressing prediction of the doctors when I left the army, I felt quite chuffed. The doctors could also see the improvement when I went for my medical and they instantly reduced my pension and suggested that I got a light part-time job. Those being the days of direct labour, I was sent to the local Civil Defence post to answer the telephone and do odd jobs. Six months later I went for my next medical. They reduced my pension yet again and told me to try something more active. On this recommendation the Ministry of Labour directed me to a job of 'National Importance' in the flax industry. The official name was *His Majesty's Norfolk Flax Establishment.*

I don't think it is widely known that King George VI was interested in botany. Long before the War he assisted in the development of a small experimental factory for the processing of flax at West Newton on the Sandringham Estate. With the coming of the War and the shortage of raw materials this small factory was taken over by the Ministry of Supply. From then on, the flax industry took off in a big way. A de-seeding station covering several acres was built at Drayton near Norwich and the surrounding land was covered with stacks which to the viewer looked like the usual straw stack. Practically every farm in Norfolk had to grow a percentage of this crop and after harvest it could either be stored on the farms or brought into the factory to be processed or stored in the stackyard until the winter months. It was harvested with a machine which pulled the flax out of the ground by its roots and passed it through a binder, not like corn with a cutter and binder.

Having more or less got my health and strength back, I was sent to Drayton in the spring of 1944 as a tractor driver. The factory, which employed about a hundred people, mostly women, was like a giant threshing machine. The straw, which was the vital part, went through the binder and was loaded onto lorries and transported to West Newton for processing. The flax was in very high demand for making parachute harnesses, hosepipes and all webbing equipment.

It was hard work for the women in the factory, most of them married with husbands who were either in the Forces or prisoners-of-war. They were very patriotic and conscious of the war effort. Several conscientious objectors were sent to work there and these women gave them a hard time. Though not as hard as being at the Front!

After a time we had a new fleet of lorries and I was promoted to lorry driver. This entailed going out to the farms all over Norfolk, stacking the sheaves on the lorry, roping down and getting back to the factory to keep up production. It was rather hazardous carting this material, not because of the traffic on the roads in those days, but because the flax was very slippery and difficult to load and transport. It had to be stacked properly to negotiate the small lanes around the Norfolk countryside.

All the materials passed over a weighbridge and as I visited this several times a day, it was not long before the young girl in the office was attracting my attention. Pauline and I began spending our lunch breaks together in the canteen. This became a regular occurrence and we found we had plenty to talk about. Pauline was a good listener as I related my knowledge of wildlife and the countryside. She apparently put all her spare time into the Girl Guide movement, being a Ranger and also helped with the young children in the Brownies. At weekends she did voluntary work at the nearby hospital which housed wounded servicemen.

We continued getting to know one another over lunch, until one day Pauline asked me for directions to an area very near my home. Apparently the Guides had a permanent camp on the estate where previously I had helped the 'keepers, and Pauline had been invited to stay at camp — cycling to work in the mornings and returning to camp at night. As the holder of a lifesaving certificate, she was to stay there during the school holidays for the younger children to enjoy swimming in the river. I took Pauline on a 'short-cut' to her destination, which was in fact the longest way round, just for the benefit of her company. It involved going over a field, along a footpath where we had to push the bikes and then over a footbridge where I had to carry them. Pauline never went that way again for on her subsequent visits to the camp, she decided the shortest way was by the main road.

After camping was over we arranged to meet one Saturday afternoon in the city and spend the afternoon and evening together. As we both worked on Saturday mornings until twelve noon, we confirmed our arrangements for the afternoon before we left. On my arrival home I found disaster had struck. My youngest brother Buddy, the baby of the family and just eight years old, had been tragically killed. Apparently he had gone up onto the heath with several other boys and they had decided to play soldiers in the sand-pit nearby. This involved digging trenches, a familiar scene in wartime. Buddy was digging away and about four foot down when the sand caved in on top of him. There was panic amongst the children and although they ran to the village for help it was to no avail. Mother and Father had gone to the cattle market as they had entered some pigs in the sale. They had to be contacted and brought home to this devastating scene. This tragedy was felt deeply by us all as we were a close family and Buddy, being the youngest, was nearest and dearest to all our hearts.

Mother, despite her anguish, was ever thoughful of all the practical things that had to be done. Somebody had to inform the relatives who lived in Norwich before it was published in the newspapers. I volunteered, not mentioning that I already had a date and was going to Norwich anyway.

Pauline met the bus as arranged and could instantly see something was amiss. After imparting my sad news, we both knew our arrangements would have to be postponed and I would have to carry on with the sad task of informing the relatives. Without hesitation Pauline said she would accompany me. I found this very gratifying to have the benefit of her company at such an unhappy time. I was very upset and couldn't find my tongue but I was glad to have her with me. It was mid-September and the days were very hot. Normally it would have been an ideal day to take a girl out, but first we had to walk to the cattle market to collect the money from the sale of the pigs. Being wartime the buses were all full and it was hopeless to even consider getting a bus on Saturdays. There was only one thing for it and that was to walk. It was two miles to our destination which we walked in the heat of the day. On the return journey we got as far as Chapelfield Gardens, where we found a seat and rested before I caught my bus and returned home to my grief-stricken family.

Pauline agreed to come out with me some other time and after this sad start we began to see one another regularly. It wasn't long before we couldn't see too much of one another. My courting days seemed to involve a lot of cycling at all hours of the night and day. I remember once coming home in the early hours of the morning and meeting my brother on the stairs as he was coming down and I was going up, I said, "Goodnight," and he said, "Good Morning." He drove a threshing turn-out and had to be on site early to get steam-up in the engine.

After a time Pauline began to stay over the weekend or I would visit her home and stay there. When Pauline came to our village, it was impossible to lodge at our house as being a big family, accommodation was very limited so she put up at the local pub. Coming out into the country was an experience for her as the pub didn't have electricity upstairs and she had to take a lighted candle to bed. Thereafter the pub became known as 'Jamaica Inn'. I think the ghostly candle light and the creaking pub sign outside the bedroom window played on her imagination! We had some lovely weekends walking on the heath and swimming in the river. On V.E. day we had a hilarious time, Mother had saved three penny pieces for the duration, for in her practical way she said, "We must have something to fall back on if we are ever bombed out." Fortunately this never happened. The large biscuit tin that had been soldered up for the duration was broken open and its entire contents spent in one day on all the beer anyone could drink. I withdrew around three o'clock in the afternoon to sleep it off in the wheelbarrow at the top of the garden, where I had the sensation somebody was pushing me around the garden.

The war with Germany now being over, we realized we had never had a holiday away from home. In the August we dived into our savings and went off to London for a week. I had an aunt who lived at Hendon and she invited us to stay. For two people who hadn't had a holiday for years, we crammed as much as possible into one week. We shopped in the West End and Petticoat Lane, visited all the sights, danced in all the night spots. When we returned on the following Sunday morning we were worn out and spent out. We stood on the forecourt of the station when we arrived in Norwich and went through the loose change in our pockets. Deciding we hadn't enough for a taxi and that our living-it-up was finished, it was back to the bus and a long walk with the suitcases.

Our courtship was not all hearts and roses, we had our ups and downs. At one time we split up but it only lasted one week as we were both thoroughly miserable. We realized we couldn't live without one another so we finally named the day.

We were married at St. Mary and St. Walston's Church at Bawburgh on the first of June, 1946. The church was crammed full of people, country people making much of these events. Prior to the wedding my mother and her army of workers had scrubbed the church floor and cleaned all the pews, before decorating it with flowers. We had over one hundred people as guests and although food rationing was still with us, it was amazing how much food appeared through knowing the friend of a friend. My mother organized the whole thing and how she must have worked to provide a sit down meal for all those people. I think they all had a convivial time. We left early in the evening with 'Just Married' all over the car and a string of old boots and tin cans trailing out the back. We had a marvellous send-off from friends and family. I was leaving them all to take up my new life and I was full of confidence for the future with Pauline by my side. After we left the reception, the city people from Pauline's family had a taste of country hospitality. The wine flowed with old Uncle Hoddy doing his clog dance and singing, "I'll never knock at the wrong street door," and as they do in the country, everybody performed their particular party piece.

Travelling was still rather a problem and the coastal resorts were still trying to get back on their feet after the War. We took a taxi to a coastal village where we stayed for a few days before I returned to resume work as a married man. A house was out of the question at this time for with everyone returning from the Forces, it was impossible to rent or buy. We lived with Pauline's parents where we had the opportunity to save towards getting a home of our own. I changed my job at the first opportunity as the flax industry was being phased out as flax was being imported again. I kept thinking of taking up gamekeeping but at this time nothing was available so I took a situation as 'ganger', looking after prisoners-of-war. For this I had to report to Kimberly Park, where the prisoners were camped. I was responsible for twenty men, to set them to work hoeing, draining, ditching and hedging on the various farms. By now I had lost all my army pension and it was gratifying to know that I was physically fit.

The prisoners-of-war were German and on the whole I got on very well with them. They were very hard-working and a lot of them were country boys, well acquainted with farm work. It was very interesting to hear of some of their war experiences and most of them spoke good English. Generally they were very self-sufficient: they had a pen at the camp which they used to rear wild rabbits, and they would also unravel sacks, pull out the threads and dye them to make slippers and shopping bags, and very good they were too. I had a dilapidated old coat in my lorry which was donkey's years old and one of them asked me if he could have it. The next time I saw it, it looked as though it had come out of Burton's window — it was immaculate. It had been unpicked, washed, turned and restored by an expert.

When we were sent to a new farm, these boys would always ask me to negotiate with the farmer for a sack of potatoes and a can of milk. Sometimes the farmer said, "They are Germans — I'm not giving them anything," to which I replied, "Please yourself, but when they hoe it's a lot better to be accurate or you can lose a lot of beet!" If they didn't get any food they used to chop out to a rhythm, at each stroke of the hoe saying, "No potatoes, no milk, no sugar beet for the bloody farmer!" This usually got results.

Once they got their milk and potatoes they really worked. Fritz was the cook, he would get a fire going and I had my lunch with them. It was good to have a hot meal during the day. On the whole they were a great bunch but occasionally a Nazi was sent to join the group, usually a trouble-maker who was passed around from gang to gang. The Nazis were the blue-eyed, blonde Aryan boys — if you asked them to do anything they would spit at you. Being tall, the prisoners called me 'Lunger,' and with my army boxing experience it didn't take me long to sort them out — and I didn't speak German either!

During the bad winter of 1947 we went snow-clearing. We dug snow from Easton Dog through to Scarning, some twelve miles away, over a period of six weeks. We dug our way out in the morning and by lunch time would have to dig our way back to the lorry. That was a very bad winter and the worst I had ever experienced.

One day when we were working on a farm a prisoner saw a rabbit in a pipe at a gateway. He immediately put a sack over the end of the pipe and poked the other end with a stick. He caught the rabbit in the sack and came to me and said, "Look Lunger, a rabbit," I replied "No, Rat." "No, rabbit" he argued. He untied the sack to prove his point and out jumped the rabbit like a jack-in-the-box. All the prisoners roared!

At this time I was still living in the city and though I worked in the country, I was finding it increasingly difficult to settle down. On Sunday mornings I got up early and cycled into the country to pick mushrooms or blackberries. At first I thought living in the city was wonderful, with shops just down the road and a hop on a bus to visit the pictures. After a time I began to feel stifled by so many houses and so many people and I realized I was not going to change from being a country boy. I followed up several leads to get a house in the country which all failed and the prospects were rather dismal. On reading of a situation advertised for a Gamekeeper/Warrener on an estate some eight miles out of the

city, I immediately applied for the situation. The prisoners were slowly being sent home and I realized I would soon be out of a job. Here too was an opportunity to get a house and the type of job I had always wanted.

The estate where the job was situated had apparently been occupied by the army during the War and now the shooting rights were let and a shooting syndicate formed. I was fortunate in getting an interview and explained all my credentials — I was too near home not to — and explained how I wanted to take up game-keeping. The boss said, "If you are honest enough to tell me, you're honest enough for the job." Pauline and I immediately hired a car and drove out to take a look at the house. We weighed all the pros and cons and decided to give it a go.

CHAPTER 5

Moreton Hall Estate

The day we moved into our new home we were up early to catch the train from the now-discarded City Station on the Midland and Great Northern Railway. The line ran from Norwich to Melton Constable and stopped at every village on the way. We left the train at Attlebridge station loaded with numerous bags and suitcases to walk the half a mile to the Lodge. As we walked, we were both very conscious of the fact that curtains were moving in the houses we passed as everybody noted the two strangers entering the village. The hedges were covered with silvery cobwebs and hoar frost, though it was only mid-October. It was the first frost of the season and bitterly cold. The house was situated at the entrance of the drive to the Hall and looked rather stately as we approached with its tall ornamental chimneys bordering a wood and overlooking the river and the park. On arrival we unlocked the massive gothic front door with an enormous key and on opening the door, the cold seemed to come to meet us. Leaving all our baggage we hastily went into the wood at the back to collect firewood. We soon had a blazing fire going in an attempt to warm up the place and thaw ourselves out. The rooms were very large, compared to what we were used to, with great high ceilings, metal window frames in stone surrounds, and concrete floors. With the river on one side and trees — which tend to hold in the damp — on the other, it

was apparent that it was going to be a mammoth job to keep the place warm. We had nowhere to sit apart from one hearth rug, so making a cup of tea, we sat together in front of the fire to await the furniture van.

We had drawn all our savings out to buy some essentials, that is, what we were allowed to buy, as all furniture, blankets, carpets and curtains were rationed and on points. After thawing out, we rolled up our sleeves and had a general clean-up and fixed the curtains. Our furniture was being delivered in the afternoon and we had plenty to do cleaning the windows and scrubbing floors. When the furniture van arrived we gave the men a hand to unload all our precious new furniture and after having a cup of tea, they were off. Later when we were trying to arrange the bedroom, we realized they hadn't left the spring to the bed, therefore we had nothing to sleep on. I hastily went to the 'phone box down the road and rang the shop but apparently they could do nothing until the next day. All we could do was put the mattress on the floor and make the bed up. So our first night in our own home was spent on the floor, but we were so tired with all the hard work and upheaval of laying lino and hauling furniture around that we didn't even notice!

The house looked quite comfortable for a first home, though a trifle bare. We had spent all our points and hadn't enough left over for rugs or carpets, so apart from one hearth rug which we had made, all the floors were covered with lino. Having no stair carpet we stained the stairs which was all right until one day Pauline decided to polish them and I slid from top to bottom. The bareness was accentuated when the great gothic front door clanged. It vibrated through the house like banging the church door. There was a pump outside in the out-house which we found you had to prime with half a gallon of water before you could get a drop out, and we had oil lamps for lights. However as this was our first home, however humble, and the first time we had been on our own since we had been married, we overlooked the lack of 'mod cons.'

We had quite a large garden bordering the wood and surrounding the house. There were two golden retrievers in pens in the garden named Ben and Dina and my job was to exercise these dogs. When I opened the pen door, they both rushed out and nearly knocked me over, then were gone. I whistled and I called but to no avail. I thought "This is a good start." It took me all the morning to walk the estate and find the pair but when I came home, they were walking to heel and coming around to the fact that I was their new master. These dogs were to prove very erratic in their behaviour and as I found out later, they were the result of bad breeding. However the boss thought they were wonderful and it was simply my job to look after them.

I soon began to realize that Pauline was having difficulty adjusting to living in the country. Born and bred in the city and being used to having everything to hand, it took some getting used to when she realized there wasn't a shop just around the corner, let alone electricity. With all her Girl Guide experience, she had been taught how to kindle a fire but somehow the art eluded her. It has taken years of teaching and chaffing on my part, with "call yourself a Girl Guide," for she just had no idea how to light a fire. This ability was very important as with no electricity, life revolved around the 'Triplex' stove which had an oven on one side and trivets in the front for cooking on the open fire. Things that I took for granted, like the correct woods to burn to get the heat in the fire for cooking, were a complete mystery to her. Though a good cook, the frustration of trying to get results from the range led to some heated moments which didn't come from the stove! But with perseverance, patience and an awfully long time, all began to fall into place.

Pauline always maintained that she loved the country. However, taking country walks on a bright spring day was one thing but being confronted with no street lights and complete darkness, the wind in the trees and the owls hooting was another thing altogether. Once the oil lamp was lit and the curtains drawn, both doors were securely locked to keep out any wandering marauders.

At my first opportunity I got the old bike out and began to survey the estate. Our house was situated at one end on the boundary, the estate continued alongside the River Wensum, through open park land, leading to a steep drive uphill through a wood which was called 'The Oven,' to the Hall and its outbuildings. The Hall was not inhabited and looked rather neglected, having been let as a furniture repository. The once-lovely gardens were all overgrown and evidence of army occupation was everywhere. All the bronze statues in the garden looked as though they had been used for rifle practice! Carrying on past the Hall there was another huge park, and beyond that the village of Ringland; turning right the road continued on to Weston Longville and Parson Woodforde country.

Ringland is one of the most beautiful spots in Norfolk; the river winds its way through the meadowland in a valley, the surrounding fields gently rising to the hills and Eve's Gap Wood which runs along the top of the heights. This whole end of the estate was surrounded by breckland which was called 'The Brecks.' It was only too obvious that the whole place was absolutely infested with rabbits. The soil was very light, and with nothing done on the estate for six years, I realized that there was a formidable task ahead to get the rabbit population down. I know it is impossible to find a contented farmer but the farmers on this estate *really* had a gripe for crop damage was apparent in every field. When walking onto the park at any time of the day, if I clapped my hands, the whole place seemed to move as the rabbits bolted for their burrows.

I had been promised help in this task and my help soon put in an appearance. He introduced himself as 'Darkie.' He was in his mid-thirties, quite small, wore breeches, rubber boots, jacket and cap with a red neckchief. He used to cycle from Norwich every day with an alsatian/labrador dog trotting by his side. This old dog amazed me. He would trot all the way from Norwich, do a hard day's rabbiting and then trot all the way home, keeping it up five days a week throughout the season.

Darkie, I soon discovered was a character. He had been on the other side of the fence at some time in his life and could tell a few tales. One day when we were rabbiting, we came across a scarecrow in a field. Darkie went over to it and eyed it up and down, looked at its raincoat, then looked at his own. Realizing that it was in better condition than his own, he proceeded to exchange it.

After surveying the estate, our first job was to get all our tools ready for the assault on the rabbit population. We ordered cartridges, traps and snares from the boss and proceeded to make a colossal number of snares.

We buried all the snares in the ground to discolour the brass and prevent it showing up in the moonlight. We then had to cut a load of elder, about six inches in diameter, sawing it into ten inch lengths, avoiding all the knots. Then, splitting these lengths, we cut several stakes to the shape of a tent peg. Cutting to this shape prevented the peg from twisting and the rabbit pulling the stake out when snared. When all the stakes were shaped, we trimmed them with a knife and placed the tips in the fire to harden them, which would prevent splitting when knocking them into hard ground. The trickers, which held the snare in position, we cut out of black hazel about nine inches long, and the thickness of a pencil, trimming a point at one end and making a split at the other to insert the wire. Making the snares up entailed tying the cord from the stake to the wire with a half hitch, at the same time pulling

the wire into a pear shape and inserting the wire into the tricker and putting the peg through the loop of the wire twice. Then they were ready to be transported for use.

Carrying about a hundred snares looped over our arms and walking along the grasslands, we selected the runs. A rabbit has a big jump and a small jump, so we inserted the tricker just before the small jump, well back from the run and at an acute angle, then positioned the loop of the snare to overhang the run about four fingers high. Setting the snare, we inserted the peg well back, kicking it in with the heel of our boot. We set these snares at considerable speed taking about one hour to place a hundred.

Setting the snares in the late afternoon meant I had to be up at daylight to cycle about two miles and inspect the snares. More often than not, there were so many rabbits that I wasn't able to transport them home on the bike. I hurdled them by cutting a slit in the skin on the back leg, inserting the other back leg in the slit, then hooked them on a bough at the edge of the wood to collect later. Several times we had to hire the estate lorry to transport them to the house. Darkie and I snared rabbits all through the summer on the meadow and grass land, as well as in the parks and in the autumn we tackled all the corn stubbles.

Darkie always arrived, while I was having a quick breakfast, and sorted out all the gear ready for a day's rabbiting. When we set off, with ferret box, rabbit spades, nets, guns and dogs, there was a sizable amount of gear to transport on bikes. We commenced with the banks and hedgerows, leaving the woods until the end of the shooting season. This entailed line ferreting for which we used male ferrets or jacks which were strong and could hold a rabbit while we dug them out. A good dog here was a great asset. Darkie's old dog told us where to turn the ferret in and on feeling the ferret strike on the end of the line, we could start digging. The ferret line was eight yards long with a red marker one foot from the ferret

and then a marker at intervals of one yard. The markings were to tell you the distance you had to dig to reach where the rabbit and ferret were holed up.

In the spring when rabbits are breeding and many of the does have young it isn't uncommon, when line ferreting, to turn the ferret into a hole and have it kicked back into your lap with incredible force. To get the old ferret back into a hole after this was nigh impossible. Darkie would swear at him and dust him with his cap but the old ferret wouldn't have any for the rest of the day!

After Christmas we made a start on the woods when we went bolting rabbits. To do this we used about six female ferrets or jills, which we cooped, that is, tied their mouths up. On turning the ferrets into the burrows, we didn't have to wait long before the rabbits bolted out of the holes. Standing back with the gun we rolled them over as they raced along in an attempt to escape. When the rabbits bolted well, the gun fire was a continual barrage. On a crisp, frosty morning with the ferrets working well, the rabbits went in all directions, bounding along with their little white tails flashing in the sunlight. We could only afford to buy old guns and it wasn't long, with this continual wear and tear, before a hole appeared in one of the barrels, which we had brazed up. I have had guns blow up in my face. These hurdle irons, as we called them, were by modern standards, unfit for use — I wouldn't fire one of them today.

Bolting rabbits day after day made us really keyed up — our reflexes were instantaneous and being so used to shooting, we very seldom missed. This had disastrous results one day when, in a high wind, Darkie's hat went bowling along. Bang! Too late! It was like a colander when he retrieved it!

We worked in one area until lunch time. After lunch we trapped all the holes that had been ferreted in the morning. The bolt holes were sealed up with newspapers, and the entrance hole into the

burrow trapped. This way we picked up the rabbits that hadn't bolted previously. At this time the rabbit would not smell humans, their scent being concealed by the smell of the ferret. The rabbit has a very keen sense of smell but rather poor eyesight.

Very often ferrets were lost when we were ferreting. If this happened we filled all the holes up, leaving the main entrance. Digging a hole two foot six inches deep with sides sloping inwards we hulked two freshly killed rabbits and left their entrails at the bottom of the hole. When the ferret came out, he was attracted by the smell and fell into the hole. Going round the traps in the evening, I collected any lost ferrets at the same time.

Of course, some days things didn't go right and the ferrets got hung up. They worked well but the rabbits would not bolt. Sometimes they seemed to take no end of punishment before they finally made a run for it. Darkie and I, with the help of the dogs, worked as a team and the rabbit population took a severe hammering day after day. We really attacked these rabbits with everything and in every way we could but even so, I was always having angry farmers at my door complaining of rabbit damage. They put in claims for rabbit damage to the boss so he in turn would get irate, so I was beginning to realize that this was a never-ending job.

I cycled miles in the course of a day — no cars in those days for 'keepers! I had problems with poachers and had to show myself, which entailed biking around the beat at all times of the night. The village policeman at Weston was very helpful, meeting up with me somewhere on the estate and we spent many a long hour together.

Shooting day was every Tuesday. The guns who belonged to the syndicate were mostly business men living some distance away. I had to arrange for the beaters which usually involved visiting the pub to recruit these boys. We didn't place sticks for the guns or plan the drives beforehand. There was quite a good stock of wild game and many suitable places to put on a good show. Most of the woods were situated on a hill, resulting in good pheasants. The partridge shoot was also very good, partridges being plentiful in the days before we got involved in intensive farming.

After the shooting season we had a rough rabbit shoot. Prior to this I cut up sacking which I soaked in renodine and two days before the shoot, I toured the estate dropping these pieces into as many rabbit holes as I could find to discourage the rabbits from entering the holes and encouraged them to 'sit rough.' Every gun had a beater and each beater had to keep count of the number of times the gun missed. At the end of the day each gun had to give the beater one penny for every miss. Darkie and I were so used to shooting rabbits that we didn't have to pay our beaters anything so they used to moan. Some of the guns had to hand over quite a lot!

I had seen rabbits in the harvest field when I was a boy but that was nothing compared with the rabbits at harvest time on this estate. When the binder had reduced the field to one small area in the middle, it would be one seething mass of rabbits.

In these early days our housekeeping was very much a hit-and-miss affair. At every opportunity Pauline would lay down her tools and accompany me when we walked all over the estate. I taught her how to read the countryside, to not just see a tree but identify what kind of tree, how it bent to the prevailing wind, also the state and the wildlife that used it, observing the droppings etc. We walked the banks of the river Wensum observing the different species of duck. We made a natural hide on the river bank to observe the heron and kingfishers hunting for food. I also taught her to shoot, first with a four-ten and then with a twelve-bore. Also to act as beater and walk a small area to drive the rabbits out for me to shoot.

When I went on my first rabbiting expedition and Pauline saw me giving the ferrets a saucer of milk before we ventured off, she eyed these creatures with great suspicion, having never seen one before. I began to find that every time I came home, it was usually to a crisis, like the time when the ferret got out of the hutch. Apparently I had failed to secure the latch when taking the ferrets out in the morning and one jumped out of the hutch and began to explore the area. The back door being open, it ventured into the hall. Pauline came out of the kitchen and being confronted by a ferret, bolted back into the kitchen and secured the door. Here she remained for some two hours listening to the patter of little feet on the lino outside. I think to her the ferret represented a man-eating tiger. The butcher saved the day when he called to deliver the meat. Pauline called him to the kitchen window and asked, "I don't suppose you can pick up a ferret?" The butcher replied, "Yes, if you've got a glove handy." Pauline found a glove and handed it to him, whereupon much to her relief and in a matter of seconds, he picked up the ferret and placed it in the hutch.

Our first son was born in the August and we named him Ivan, very apt as it turned out, as we always called him Ivan the Terrible. He kept Pauline very busy as we had lots of problems with him. We found we got plenty of advice from doctors, nurses and mothers on both sides, but after a succession of sleepless nights, Pauline threw all the good advice away and reared him on baby food which she fed him with a spoon. It wasn't until years after when his second teeth were forming when it was pointed out that he had a deformed lower jaw. Remembering all the trouble we'd had with feeding at this time, we realized this had been the trouble all along. When he reached adulthood he underwent a marvellous operation to reconstruct his lower jaw which rectified all these problems. However he was a lovely little chap and we were very happy to have him.

On our first outing with Ivan in the pram we walked to the village fête at Weston Longville where I entered the 'bowling for the pig' competition which, much to my amazement, I won. What to do with this poor little pig put us in a bit of a quandary. I received offers to buy it but after some thought decided I would keep it. I brought it home under my arm, riding my bike at the same time, which took a bit of doing — it was only two months old and wriggled and squeaked all the way home. I kept it in a box while I made a makeshift sty out of bales of straw and netting until I could provide a more permanent shelter. As the house was situated on the outskirts of a wood, the garden where I built the sty penetrated the wood. After a few days and while I was away on the estate, the pig unfortunately got out. I think Pauline had a little wild boar hunt on her own trying to catch the pig. When I returned home the pig was still running free, playing hide and seek amongst the trees. With the aid of my dog and a lot of manoeuvering, we managed to catch him. I realized he had outgrown his temporary shelter and had to build a permanent sty.

As food was rationed we applied for a food ration to feed the pig. Boiling potatoes and adding barley meal, we decided we would fatten it up and have it slaughtered. We had to apply for permission to do this and lose our bacon ration for six months. When the day came that I decided the pig was fat enough, I contacted the local butcher and arranged for it to be slaughtered. Much to my amazement the butcher said, "You won't have to bring the pig up here, get the copper going and I will call in my van Monday morning." Poor Billy the pig had been treated as a pet by Pauline; he would squeak over his sty and she would scratch his head and in return he closed his eyes in sheer bliss. It didn't suit her at all that the butcher was to exterminate poor Billy at all — let alone on our premises.

When the butcher arrived I had the copper boiling as promised. Mr Bland the butcher, I had known since I was a boy. He had been badly shell-shocked during the First World War making his limbs fly all over the place in jerking movements. He had problems with holding a knife still, therefore he held this instrument between his teeth, giving him the appearance of a pirate in a boarding party. He was very efficient and soon had poor Billy processed. He wouldn't take any payment for killing and jointing the meat, "All I want is the belly and the jot," he said, and he was quite happy to receive this. At this time meat was rationed to such a degree that we only qualified for a joint at week-ends. We had one feed of roast pork with all the trimmings but somehow our hearts weren't in it. We gave away the rest to friends and relations, resulting in our losing our bacon ration for six months to no avail!

On my cycle tours of the estate I had reason to call at Ringland quite often as poaching seemed to be prolific in this area. There were two public houses in Ringland, The Swan and The Union Jack. Joe Seaman, a retired 'keeper, kept The Union Jack. I loved to call on Joe and have a natter as he had a wealth of knowledge about estates and gamekeeping. He used to tell me of the duck decoy on Fritton Lake which is on the Somerleyton Estate and how he worked this duck decoy. Little did I know that long after he died I would be walking in his footsteps. He also used to work on the estate that I was then on and put me right on one or two matters. He was a good old boy.

All animal feed was still rationed at this time, and it was impossible to rear any pheasants. I did make an attempt to rear a few under hens using the old method of feeding the pheasant chicks on boiled rabbit meat and hard boiled eggs. I didn't really have a lot of time for the finer points of gamekeeping as my days were full in pursuit of rabbits.

I had a friend in the cowman employed on the next-door farm who dropped in at odd times for a chat as he was interested in dog training and gamekeeping in general. One day he brought me several turkey eggs. I put these under hens and succeeded in hatching twelve. As meal was rationed or unobtainable Pauline and I collected nettles which we chopped finely to mix with chopped hard-boiled eggs to feed them. We reared the twelve. When they were old enough to leave the hen, they wandered all over the park and wood, enjoying their roaming commission. I trained them to go to perch in the yew tree in our garden. As Christmas approached I anticipated making a good return on these turkeys as food was still rationed and in short supply.

I was very disturbed to hear on the radio about all the poultry poaching that was going on in the area. My birds were very near the road and plainly visible. I decided nobody was going to steal my birds so I put a trip wire right around the house and connected it to a large galvanized bungalow bath which hung on the wall outside, below which was a concrete floor. I took my gun to bed with me and told Pauline that if that bath fell to the floor, she would have to watch out because I would fire old 'Betsy' out of the bedroom window.

I had my trap set for about a week. One night I called to see old Joe down at The Union Jack and being late home, I came into the garden hell-for-leather. I forget about the trip, went flying, and the bungalow bath came off the wall with a clatter. Pauline came rushing out thinking the poachers had arrived, only to find me truly snared!

While I was at Moreton I heard about the annual Gamekeeper's Clay Pigeon Shoot at Taverham and as I fancied myself a good shot, I thought I would take part in this event. Lunch was provided free — we just had to pay for the cartridges and enter the events. This was specifically for gamekeepers and the four top scores in the morning would compete against well-known estate owners in the afternoon. I had the privilege of performing in this event. It was a great day out, mixing with all the gamekeeping fraternity and meeting old friends. It usually followed the same pattern, good shooting in the morning until they went into the beer-tent at lunch time, diabolical after!

News would travel on these occasions about all the different estates and owners. The season would also be discussed and the different methods of rearing and so forth. I would say ninety-five per cent of the 'keepers in Norfolk and Suffolk attended this shoot. It was a marvellous turn-out. The gamekeeping fraternity has been greatly reduced now, only one being employed where there were once five. Mixing with this crowd was a great education and I was beginning to realize I was doing two jobs for the price of one.

It was extremely hard work trying to get on top of the constant rabbit problems. I seemed to be working twenty-four hours a day, seven days a week. I asked the boss for a bonus on the rabbits we caught and he came up with one farthing a head which Darkie and I had to share between us. However we carried on. We had another two part-time warreners and between us, in two-and-a-half years, we killed 28,500 rabbits.

My son was nearly two years old at this time and constantly poorly, which we realized was due to the house being near the river and very cold. We decided that it wasn't advisable to spend another winter in that environment and that it was necessary to find another situation.

I didn't have to look very far, about two miles in fact. Great Witchingham Hall needed a 'keeper and I decided to enquire about it.

My father, resplendent in the uniform of the Royal Horse Guards, the Blues.

(Above) Frank, left, on a trip to Great Yarmouth with his brothers in 1929.

(Left) The Author with Major.

(Left) Trooper 305589, Cullum D. F., 1941.

(Below) Frank and Pauline, photographed soon after they met at Drayton.

The Lodge, Attlebridge.

(Left) Our Wedding Day 1946.

Great Witchingham Hall.

(Right) Raising pheasant chicks at West Raynham. In the top photograph the chicks are about eight weeks old and the hens are in the coops. In the lower photograph the chicks have reached about twelve weeks and the coops have been removed.

Keepers and friends at West Raynham. Author, extreme right.

Mill Covert, West Raynham.

1959. Ivan and Paul with Pauline's parents. The dog is a half-bred Irish water spaniel, named 'Putty' by Paul.

With Stephen and Pauline at Somerleyton.

At Morston, 1960, with our third son Stephen.

Our two eldest boys, Ivan aged eight and Paul, six.

Ivan, now aged twelve on Fritton Lake during the time that I was in charge of the decoys there.

(Above) Somerleyton Hall.

(Below) Decoy at Fritton, about 1911.

With the grandchildren at the Christening of Stephen's daughter, Rachel, in 1985.

CHAPTER 6

Great Witchingham Hall

I arrived for my appointment with the Head Keeper, Harry Jacobs. We had a talk about my past experiences and when Harry was satisfied with my background, we went down to the Hall to see the squire, William James Barry.

He was then an elderly man but very astute — here was an old English gentleman, a marvellous shot and a very keen fisherman. We talked about the estate in general and the state of the wild stock. When I had accepted the situation, he explained about the beat for which I was to be responsible. Apparently it was mostly a partridge beat, and considerably smaller than my previous estate.

I didn't look at the house as anything would be an improvement on our present accommodation. I took Harry's word that it was clean and presentable. So we moved to Great Witchingham at the end of February 1950. The house was situated about one mile from the Hall, smaller than the previous one, compact, high and dry. We soon felt the difference of living away from the river. Somedays when we had fog or mist in our former house it was very dense and didn't clear all day. We had always kept good fires but the atmosphere was so damp the mirrors ran with water. We worked all the weekend on this house and we were well pleased with the result when everywhere looked very neat and tidy.

With everything straight on the home front, Harry acquainted me with my beat, spending a considerable time explaining all the facts. At this stage I didn't know too much about partridges and realizing this, he educated me. Here began a long association with Harry. He had endless patience and we were to spend hours together discussing the habits of the wildlife. After my previous situation which was all work, I now had time to stand and stare and take in all the finer points of 'keepering.

The estate was a 'sporting' estate, with lovely woods for displaying pheasants, and a considerable amount of meadow land bordering the river Wensum, which ran through the estate, and which also formed the squire's trout stream.

I soon had all my vermin traps established for this estate had been well kept and therefore pests were well under control. I spent any spare time I had observing the habits of the English partridge, which was a source of wonder to me.

Prior to my first nesting season, Harry presented me with a map of my beat, and told me to mark all the partridge nests I found on the map and show him my entries every two weeks.

Apparently the squire kept a map at the Hall of all the nests recorded from the information we supplied.

I took the first map I completed to Harry as instructed, showing nine partridge nests in one small hedge. Harry thought this was too good to be true and decided to make an inspection himself. Satisfied, he reported back to the squire who said he would like to see them too, on the following Monday.

Come Monday morning the squire arrived at our house in his old Armstrong Siddley coupé, chauffeur-driven. I climbed aboard this sumptuous car which was more like a charabanc and at his command to the chauffeur, "Carry on, Picket," we drove off. When we arrived at the spot, we left the car and proceeded quietly to the hedge. I had all the nests variously marked, never the same twice. If I used twigs they were dead ones as to mark with a twig in leaf is a sure give-away because when the leaves wilt they make an obvious marker. I varied my markers with stones and clods, mostly different stones. When the squire had inspected the nests, he was amazed. After this phenomenon, Harry called and said that he wanted to show me how to dress a partridge nest.

When a partridge makes a nest, it is just a scrab in the earth and very shallow, so that more often than not it has to be deepened to prevent eggs rolling out. The partridge lines the nest with leaves and every time she lays an egg she covers it with fillings such as dry leaves. This is to camouflage the nest against winged predators such as magpies or crows. Before the hen sits she removes these fillings and puts them in the bottom of the nest and arranges her eggs in a compact circle. When this happens, you know the hen is ready to go down. Harry demonstrated how to approach the nest at this time, removing the eggs and fillings, making a small hole in the centre big enough to take a cartridge case. He then filled a cardboard cartridge case with Jeyes Fluid and inserted it in the hole, lightly covering it with soil and carefully putting the fillings and eggs back. The Jeyes Fluid seeped out of the container during the incubation period and prevented intrusion or interference from moles. The weasel uses a mole run and he can cause considerable damage, so in this way you could deter two predators by the same method.

Early one Sunday morning, the first of June, I was touring my tunnel traps when I heard a shot come from the direction of the main road. I dashed off on my bike and as I approached the bridge on the main road I recognized my poacher. He was cycling along and every time his leg went round with the pedal I could see the tip of a four-ten showing underneath his coat. Although he didn't recognize me — I was a small boy when he last saw me — I knew him from my Father's associations in his poaching days.

When he had passed me and continued along the road towards Norwich, I immediately made for the police house which was about a mile in the same direction. I acquainted the policeman with the facts and he drove his car out of the garage and I directed him along the lane which ran beside the main road. We then turned right onto the road and there was our poacher coming towards us. When we stopped him he called me a few names and said, "You crafty so-and-so, you wouldn't have caught me if you had come from behind." He had a number of pheasants and partridges plus a four-ten gun in his possession. I returned home thoroughly dejected and disgusted when I thought of the partridges I had lost. In all my poaching experience I had always been brought up to respect the nesting season. I found it hard to accept anybody poaching at this time of the year.

I had my breakfast but all the time I was worried about a partridge that I knew was due to hatch near the main road. I wondered if she was one of the birds that had been poached. I paid her a visit every day and this particular morning I couldn't wait to get back to her to see if all was well. I approached the nest with the sun shining on to her, quietly concealed myself, and to my amazement saw the hen with the cock bird by her side talking to one another. Presently she put her head under her wing and pulled out a chick, which she passed onto the cock and he in turn proceeded to mother it. The hen bird then snuggled down lower onto the nest and the same thing happened again at intervals. All the time this was going on they were keeping up a constant conversation with one another. I was quite relieved my poacher hadn't found them, as it was the earliest I had known a partridge to hatch. I have asked other 'keepers on my travels but I've never found anybody who could match this as hatching usually takes place about the third week in June. French partridges are entirely different from the English. They pair off in the same way but when they lay their eggs, they leave them for a considerable time. Day after day I have observed a nest and thought the hen had forsaken it as the eggs were turning green. Then suddenly, much to my amazement, I would find that the hen had gone down, and like English partridges, they are very good mothers. They do not cover the eggs with fillings but leave the nest uncovered, laying a dull spotted egg which is easily blended in with their natural surroundings. They make much more noise than their English counterparts and in the early mornings, find somewhere high up, from which to constantly 'preach' to one another!

When partridge shooting, the English birds fly well, whereas the French ones prefer to keep their feet on the ground, and will run for a considerable distance. Once you get them up they fly well and the coveys split more easily than the English birds. But after running for a distance on heavy land, the soil balls up under their feet and prevents them from flying.

Every month I had to call at the Hall and see the squire. He wanted to know how the birds were hatching, the amount of vermin and about the season in general. Squire Barry went salmon fishing in May and for days prior to leaving, he was out on the lawn with his rod, practising his casting. He put matchboxes all around the lawn as targets to place the fly — he really had this down to a fine art.

On coming home he brought us a piece of fresh salmon. We had never seen, cooked or eaten this before. It looked delicious and rather than spoil it, I enlisted the help of the cook at the Hall on how to cook it. We thoroughly enjoyed it.

Our second son Paul was born in the October, another fine boy, and as we were now experienced parents we had no problems. Pauline's days were extremely busy with two small children to look after. Becoming more proficient in the art of housekeeping in the country, the only crises now were the everyday ones associated with rearing two children. Ivan was still poorly at times and after a bad bout of whooping cough, he looked a poor little chap. We lived one mile from the local railway station and during the summer months Pauline often took him on the train to Cromer, just to sit on the beach for him to get the sea air. Those were the days of the steam train which held a great attraction for him and whenever we passed a level crossing we always had to wait for a train.

With the arrival of the shooting season, Harry and I walked the estate, planning all the drives and positioning the shooting pegs for the guns to 'stand.' He would then acquaint the squire on the preparations for the day. Only good guns were invited and the accent was on quality not quantity. When we drove the pheasants from the woods onto the low lying meadow land, they would be up there like starlings and could the squire crack them down! He was a marvellous shot. The guns would all pile into the old Armstrong Siddley and travel from stand to stand. At the end of the day, all the game was taken to the game larder at the Hall where it was hung to await the arrival of the game dealer. This was an excellent shoot with good guns who all tipped well to show their appreciation of a good day. After every shoot Harry entered the game larder, took everything from his pockets and laid it out on the table, remarking, "They have treated us very well today." Then he always split everything down the middle which I greatly appreciated.

After the shooting season we had to tackle the rabbits. Harry and I did the woods and usually left the hedges to the men employed by the tenant farms who liked a day's rabbiting. We were paid a bonus on the number of rabbits killed, the estate finding the cartridges. Here, again, Harry split everything two ways.

I have always been an early bird in the mornings. In the season I had to get around the traps early and on a normal day, I toured the beat before breakfast as it was easier to take stock at an early hour. One midsummer morning I left my garden gate to cycle into the village when I met the gardener making his way to the

Hall. He was a real old Norfolk character with his back bent to the spade. He shouted and jerked a thumb towards the village, "Mornin' Frank, you want to look over the rectory fence as you go past. There's a couple of naked Swedes flittin' about all over the place." I really couldn't understand what he was on about and just waved my hand in acknowledgement. When I reached the rectory I could hear music playing and as I passed, I glanced over the fence. There was the rector's daughter with a friend, both about sixteen years old, clad only in a G-string and performing Greek dancing on the lawn. I carried on my way but I had to laugh at the old boy's "couple of naked Swedes." He apparently had taken a good look!

Our neighbours in the house next door to us had a young family and were very amiable. Cups of tea passed over the fence which made life more agreeable for Pauline, as our former house had been very lonely. However, come the rearing season, next doors' old ginger tom went missing and there was a terrific hue and cry. Naturally I got the blame and our relationship became rather hostile after this catastrophe. I made no comment on the accusation. Pauline read the riot act and I still made no comment. Being a small community the news got around that Billy's ginger tom had gone missing. When I called in the local some days later all the boys started to sing, "I TAWT I SAW A PUDDY CAT A-CREEPIN' UP ON ME! I still made no comment!

One morning at about 11 o'clock, I was walking along a field bordered by a wood when I heard a rustling and scurrying in the undergrowth which attracted my attention. I was amazed to see a doe rabbit chasing a stoat. The muck was flying as the stoat threaded the fence with the doe rabbit on his heels, he was running for his life. To see stoats chase rabbits is a common occurrence but I had never seen the situation in reverse. Another day when walking over the bridge not far from the Hall I witnessed an otter swimming in broad daylight. I immediately stopped and surveyed this scene. After a time he caught a fish and went to the bank and proceeded to eat it. When I have been about at night, I have heard the otters whistling on the river bank but I had never seen one catch a fish in broad daylight before.

My father-in-law was a keen freshwater fisherman and he always came to stay for the holidays with us. At night he enlisted my help to go 'babbing' for eels. On one of these expeditions, we came to what we thought was the water's edge and commenced 'babbing.' In no time at all we had a bathful and had to pack up. Father-in-law said, "We will come here again tomorrow night, mark this spot with a stick." When we went to the same spot on the next night we found the stick but no water. The stick was in the middle of the meadow! Apparently there had been a thunderstorm some hours prior to our fishing and we had been 'babbing' in the overflow from the river.

A tenant farmer on the estate had a flock of pedigree chickens on the stubble near the low meadows. When he moved them in after shacking on the stubble he left behind a pedigree Rhode Island Red cockerel. I saw the farmer several times, one day stopping for a chat. I told him he had left a cockerel behind and he said, "I know, I can't catch him. If you can catch him, you can have him." I thought he was a handsome bird and would like him to grace my chicken run. One afternoon as the light was beginning to fade I saw this wily old bird go to perch in a crab-apple tree so I noted the spot and decided to go and get him when it was dark.

It was a pitch black night when I made my way up the hedge and found the crab-apple tree but as I was feeling my way through the bushes I put my hands out in front of me to protect my face when all of a sudden I froze — my hands touched something cold and clammy. It breathed on me and in my fright and panic I struck out and hit something hard. It snorted and I realized it was a bullock!

When I recovered from this, I looked up and could discern the cockerel sitting on a bough of the tree. I reached up and realizing he was out of my reach, worked my way to the end of the bough which I proceeded to pull down to my level. I was just going to reach out to grab the cockerel's legs when he decided to relieve himself — it went in my eye and down my face! Nevertheless I hung on to him and brought him home. When I came into the kitchen I blinked because of coming in from the dark. I triumphantly held the cockerel aloft and said to Pauline "I got him," to which she promptly replied, "Yes, it looks as if he got you too!"

All in all, it was a pleasure to work on this estate but it was apparent the squire was aging. He loved going pigeon-shooting so Harry selected him a spot and put the coys out, but his eyesight was failing. Seeing a friend in London, he explained the frustration of his difficulty in shooting. His friend loaned him a pair of spectacles which immediately improved his vision so that he decided to order a pair for himself. When he came home complete with new specs, he ordered Harry to put the coys out — he was going after the pigeons. Harry left him in the Big Wood. Going back later he could see a pile of spent cartridges on the ground but no pigeons. The squire blamed the cartridges, but standing beside him for a time, Harry observed that when he shot, the birds were three times out of range of the gun. Harry asked to look at the pigeons through the spectacles and on doing so, observed that the glasses were so powerful that the pigeons looked like turkeys and were way out of range!

It was a very sad day when Squire Barry died, in July 1952. Unfortunately the estate came under the hammer and we had to consider moving again. It had been a great pleasure to work with Harry Jacobs for he was straightforward and honest and Squire Barry was a good sportsman and a gentleman.

While the estate was being prepared for auction, I answered an advertisement in 'The Gamekeeper and Countryside' for a situation on the Suffolk border. I didn't get a reply, although a few days later, a farmer turned up on my door-step. He was the answer to my letter.

Had I been older and wiser, I wouldn't have gone any further with this interview. I have learnt since that to go along with all the procedures on both sides is very necessary when applying for a situation. I suppose it is a gamble on both sides to make sure you have the right person. However, having two sons by this time, I was very anxious not to be out of work and decided, at his invitation, to go along and have a look at his estate. During his visit he went along to see Harry to check up on my references and Harry told him that I was worthy of a better situation than he was offering. However, I decided 'nothing ventured nothing gained,' I would go along and look at the estate.

I didn't have any transport. I had to borrow a motor-cycle and side-car and find a nursemaid for the two boys and eventually we arrived to view the place. They made us very welcome and we were shown over the estate. It consisted of five farms, very heavy land with great ditches bordering the fields, a few small woods and the shoot relying on kale, sugar beet, etc. The wages were much better than I had been getting and the house was an olde-worlde Suffolk cottage with a lovely garden and orchard.

The owner required some rearing of pheasants and shooting regularly throughout the winter, plus killing the vermin. We decided we would take the situation and while the house was being altered, my new boss loaned me a car to start work, journeying from Great Witchingham every day. The place was over-run with rats, there being numerous piggeries about the place. I set to work on these, baiting and poisoning to clean the place up. I had vermin traps going at the same time and all went exceptionally well until we moved into the house. Then things changed.

In the evenings I was apparently expected to do some chauffeuring, which didn't go down very well. The man's attitude was beginning to spell out to me that I had made the biggest mistake of my life. He had taken the trouble to check on me, but being very naive, I hadn't bothered to check on him. It was evident that we weren't going to see eye-to-eye, for the type of thing he would do was take an unleashed dog up on the rearing field. I had hundreds of young pheasants in runs. The poor birds would band themselves together on the netting with fright and cut themselves to pieces. This didn't go down very well either.

It was a very anxious time as moving house with a family wasn't very easy. Finding ourselves miles from family and friends, we were thoroughly miserable. The only thing I want to remember about living there was the day I called to Pauline to come outside. Two gentlemen were passing one another in the road outside the house, one named Mr Giddup and the other Mr Gotobed!

I soon realized the situation here was intolerable so when I saw an advertisement for a 'keeper on a North West Norfolk estate, I decided to apply. I went to see the Head Keeper on the Raynham estate, Jack Batten, who spent a considerable amount of time with us showing us round. I was very interested but also very cautious. I didn't want to make another mistake.

We were happy until we came to the house which was situated about three-quarters of a mile from the main road down a rough roadway, completely on its own and bordered by a massive wood. The place looked rather neglected and very rural. Jack left us to talk it over and we again weighed all the pros and cons and decided to give it a go.

When the removal van came to collect our furniture on the day we left Suffolk, we had lived there one year to the day. When I gave the driver instructions to our new destination he said, "Oh, you mean 'Mill Covert,' I've been there scores of times." Pauline and I looked at one another, our hearts sank, and we said, "Oh dear!"

CHAPTER 7

West Raynham

The 'keeper's house at West Raynham adjoined the wood and both were known as Mill Covert. That it ever was a mill is a debatable point, but it had all the characteristics of a mill, being built of flint and brick with the end part of the house hexagonal. This was the sitting room, and it was encircled by a verandah with pillars at the edge supporting the room above. This was a bedroom, circular in shape and access to this room was by its own stairs which were a continuation of the main staircase. As this room was separate from the main part of the house, we didn't use it as a bedroom. We called it Nelly's room! The living room and kitchen, with bedrooms above, were built on the side of the hexagon shape and all in all it did give the appearance of once being a mill.

On our arrival we found that, as promised, it was clean and freshly decorated, giving us a head start in getting unloaded and settled in. It was mid-September and we were enjoying an 'Indian summer' after a very unsettled summer season.

The next morning we had a chance to walk outside to survey our surroundings. The wood was on two sides of the house, a meadow faced the sitting room and on the other side was a field where the ground inclined sharply. When negotiating the lane bordering this field, if you looked down you could see the chimneys and roof of the cottage in the low. We had already reached the conclusion that life here was very rural compared with anywhere we had lived before. Walking out onto the meadow, we discovered that it was covered with mushrooms. We gathered a load of these and had some with our breakfast. The first thing that struck us was how quiet it was, being miles from anywhere. The only noises were bird sounds that came from the wood.

Under my conditions of employment, I received a basic farm-worker's pay, plus all the rabbits and hares I could kill. The estate was shot one day per week throughout the season. Apart from this and working under Jack Batten, the Head Keeper, I could get on and do my own thing. I had to buy all my own equipment for dealing with the rabbits but one of the reasons for my coming here was that I could see a good return on these conditions.

Having had great experience with the rabbit population, I soon had the old snares made up and pegged down on the grasslands. I invested in a .22 rifle and with this I was out at daybreak to shoot a load of rabbits; the same at dusk. We had nowhere to store the rabbits until the game dealer came round so I made a box for this purpose with air holes and lowered it down the well in the garden to keep them cool.

We had arrived at the beginning of the shooting season so I didn't have long to take stock. The old bike was brought out again and I was soon cycling here, there and everywhere. Saturday shooting, Sunday morning picking up. We planned the shoot and put the sticks out one day during the week. The estate was in ideal pheasant country, lovely woods where you could get some really high pheasants. I really enjoyed the good quality guns and good quality birds. There were four beats on the estate and an excellent lake, giving a good duck shoot. Our days were very busy, sometimes loading for His Lordship or Her Ladyship on other estates. It was a great education to travel about and see what kind of day other 'keepers could put on.

We once went to shoot in Surrey where the beaters consisted of four men and twelve terriers. I was rather apprehensive as to the dogs' behaviour should a hare or rabbit put in an appearance. Anyhow, they seemed to be under control and it went off remarkably well. With the cost of beaters today, I have often wondered if this practice should be exploited more on big estates as I was rather impressed with the day's shooting they put on.

After a time, with the extra money the rabbits were bringing in, we began to feel the benefit of moving and could put a little by for a rainy day, which we felt compensated for the house being so very isolated. No tradesmen called, apart from the grocery man once a week. We had a box at the top of the loke for bread, milk, mail and newspapers to be left. Sometimes we left our shoes there when it was muddy, walking the loke in our rubber boots and changing when we got to the top. We found winter time diabolical. Many is the time we had to dig a single track through the snow up to the box.

We made sure we were always stocked up with fuel, which meant getting out the cross-cut saw and doing-it-yourself by the light of a hurricane lamp. We had oil lamps for lights but after a time we did indulge ourselves with a calor gas cooker — we got so fed up with wrestling with the coal-fired range for if the wind didn't lie in the right direction, everything was underdone or as black as your hat!

The only contact we had with the outside world was the wireless, which we ran on batteries. It was all right when the battery was new but not up to much when you wanted to hear a boxing match and it was getting weak!

Pauline's activities were with the children most of the time. We both felt it was lovely to rear children in the heart of the countryside. We taught them how to take an interest in country life, they kept rabbits, we kept ducks and chickens and they loved the dogs. Paul at five years old fancied himself as a dog handler. We had a house pet called 'Putty,' a half-bred Irish water spaniel which was given to us by a friend when Paul was one year old. The pair of them had grown up together and were inseparable. Paul took in every detail when I trained my labradors on the meadow outside the house. Very often he would take my whistles and take Putty on the meadow and try to put her through the paces I put my dogs through. Much to our amusement Putty would go along with him for a little while and then decide she had had enough. Paul was left still blowing his whistle and turning very red in the face with frustration while Putty looked the other way and decided to have a scratch. Both the boys loved to come with me at every opportunity I could take them. In the evenings before they went to bed Pauline always read to the children and selecting books from the village library, she always managed to find something interesting and exciting but limited them to just one chapter per night. They absorbed every word and when the chapter was finished, would plead for another as children do, but the tale continued the next night. Sometimes I would listen to these stories with as much interest as the children and I would be as eager as them to hear the next episode.

When we sat quietly at night reading by the light of the oil lamp, we had our own 'Tom and Jerry show.' We were constantly plagued by mice. A mouse — we named him Victor — would make an appearance from a hole in the skirting. The dog, asleep on the hearth, suddenly got the scent of the mouse and dashed across the room. Victor went back into the hole and the dog, travelling at speed, braked and slid on the polished floor, colliding with the wall. Sniffing around the hole, the dog stood guard for a time, then getting bored he lay down with one eye open which eventually closed and he was fast asleep. When he had dozed off, out came Victor again and performed a few capers in front of the

old dog. Abruptly the dog would waken and 'snap,' but Victor always made it back to his hole for a repeat performance the next night!

We survived our first winter in this isolated spot. The weather, we found, was much harsher and very changeable, coming in from the Wash. Even in summer the sea mists would roll in. The country was wide open and there was nothing to stop the harsh winter winds. We had a wind frost which seemed to last for weeks — it was so cold the eggs froze in the chickens' nests. In March I went pigeon-shooting and stood at the edge of a young plantation. Around me were the open fields and a strong March wind was blowing with wintry showers. I happened to look towards the open country and saw what looked like a huge funnel of smoke dancing towards me at a terrific pace. I had seen small 'twisters,' or 'Rogers' as we called them but never anything like this. I threw myself flat on the ground just before it passed me. The trees in the wood were bent completely over to one yard from the ground; if they hadn't been young saplings they would all have been uprooted.

At Christmas we went to the Hall for our first hunt meeting which was held on Boxing Day. There was a large turnout as always for this occasion. We followed the hounds for a time then, like everybody else, went to the Greyhound Pub for the kill!

A lot of old characters used to come from miles around to attend this event. One old chap was small and dressed in his Sunday-best hard hat, breeches, boots and buskins which were highly polished. After one or two jars he was well away and proceeded to undress to the song *This Old Coat of Mine*. He divested himself of his garments one at a time, coming down to his immaculate boots and buskins. When he took the boots off he hadn't got any socks on and his feet were as black as coal!

During the long winter evenings I set myself the task of making a rabbit net. I sat for hours making yards and yards of net, at the same time visualizing all the rabbits I was going to catch with it, but when I had completed it, tragedy struck. One morning I walked out of the back door and was confronted with my first myxomatosis rabbit, sitting with his back up and all the tell-tale signs that were to become so familiar. Within a few days, everywhere around us was beginning to stink with the smell of rotting carcasses. This was a tragedy for us 'keepers because our wages were based on the sale of the rabbits and it was obvious we were going to be reduced to farmworkers' basic pay. It wasn't very long before we were dipping into our savings to make ends meet.

The weather that summer was very bad, the harvest was dismally late and help was needed to get it in. All the 'keepers were enlisted to help out on the combines for which we were paid extra. We were harvesting until the first week in November and the corn, what there was of it, was black and in a filthy state.

Eventually one of the 'keepers left, and his job and wages were divided among the three of us who remained, which gave us a little more scope to carry on. Without the rabbits we had more time to concentrate on shooting, preparing rides in the woods, etc.

In the springtime I had all my vermin traps going, inspecting these early in the morning before breakfast and then reporting to the Head Keeper to help out with the rearing. It was at this time of the year that I went down with a bad bout of 'flu. I was always up and away at daybreak because to get round all the traps before breakfast involved a good two to three miles' walking over some pretty rough terrain. This particular morning I couldn't get out of bed, my head was spinning and I felt dreadful. There was panic stations in the house as it is most important for this job to be done. Pauline, now a seasoned 'keepers assistant, donned wellies and as Ivan knew where all the traps were, they both set off to do the rounds. At the first trap they came to, they were confronted by a huge rat which bared its teeth at them in a frightening way.

Pauline paused and said she would have to go back and get the gun, when Ivan went to the hedge and found a stout stick which he used in a very efficient manner. Pauline felt quite relieved and also amazed as Ivan took charge and she realized he hadn't missed a thing when accompanying me on my rounds. They carried on and sprung all the traps until I was well enough to get back to work. Pauline had no problems with country life now. If I was away shooting, she would look after the chickens and ducks, exercise and feed the dogs, also get the bag over her shoulder and feed the pheasants in the woods. The land was very heavy and in wet weather it was heavy going, walking the fields and rides in the woods. The cooking she took in her stride, preparing and cooking pigeons for a pigeon pie, or plucking ducks and roasting them. I could now leave all the preparations and cooking to her. All the country dishes were tried and tested in our house. I grew all the vegetables for ours was a good garden with apple trees and we had everything in season.

We had several American servicemen living nearby who intro-duced themselves and wanted to know if they could participate in any 'huntin',' as they called it. These boys thoroughly enjoyed getting away from the camp and having a little shoot. We took them pigeon and rook-shooting and they were very keen, although sometimes a little trigger-happy! Sometimes we had a clay pigeon shoot amongst ourselves with a barbecue and we had some good times together. My yearly visit to the Gamekeepers' Clay Pigeon Shoot now changed venue from Taverham to Cambridge. I travelled to Cambridge on the train and there met up with the 'keepers from Sandringham and other estates.

After the shooting season, our first job was to catch the hen pheasants to put in the aviary. We caught these in coops positioned at different places around the estate, catching twelve cocks to every hundred hens, turning them into the aviary. This was a huge netted area with plenty of cover inside for the pheasants to feel at home, and being open-topped wild cocks flew in as well to mate with the hens. For a time they were left to settle down and we started collecting eggs about the first week in April. In the meantime we prepared all the sitting-boxes, building a bank three feet by two feet and three feet high. We piled the soil in a heap to form this bank, putting a layer of Jeyes Fluid in at every foot. The reason for building a bank and putting the nest boxes on top was to protect the hens from flooding if there was a severe thunderstorm, and also to stop moles from undermining. It also relieved the back-breaking job when taking off the sitting hens every day. We bought all the sitting hens locally, putting them down on dummy eggs for three days for a trial period before putting them on the pheasants' eggs. The nests were made of meadow hay, twisted into a bond eighteen inches long and making a ring, into the centre of which we inserted a pad of hay. This could be replaced if the nest became soiled without upsetting the nest. We put twenty-one pheasant eggs to a nest. Once the hens were down, we had them off for feeding every morning, having prepared a site for this purpose complete with tethering sticks and drinkers. One drinker was in the middle with the tethering sticks surrounding it which enabled the birds to drink, eat and relieve themselves. While the hens were feeding, we inspected the nests, cleaned them if necessary and turned the eggs. When replacing the hens we always worked to a pattern to make sure the correct hen went back on her own nest. All now being returned to the nests, the whole area was thoroughly cleansed and sanded ready for the next day. During the last week before hatching, we sprinkled the nest daily with a little warm water using a watering-can with a rose.

When the chicks hatched off and were dry, we put them in a box and the hens in a crate and took them to the rearing field. This was all prepared beforehand with coops and runs and once installed, we moved them every day onto fresh grass, making sure that the runs stood level to avoid losing any chicks.

At six weeks old they were moved again, this time into the woods to position them on a ride. Always moving at night, we transported the hen and chicks together in the coop to give them a chance to settle down before releasing them in the morning. We set the chicks free but the hens remained in the coop to continue mothering and holding the birds in the area. When performing this operation we started at the end of the ride working backwards, lifting the boards on the coops gradually, watering and feeding at the same time, all with the minimum of noise so at not to disturb the birds now that they had their freedom.

Once the birds were in the woods, a constant vigil had to be maintained against any predators such as foxes or winged vermin, carrion crows and tawny owls etc. From then on all through the summer and autumn, these birds would be fed at the same time every day. This is the only way to keep pheasants successfully, a liberal amount of straw on the ride and a good feed, always on time.

When it came to driving pheasants over the guns, nobody could write a manual on how to do this in practice. All the functions governing presentation of good birds have to be considered at the time. The factors change from season to season with the change in cropping plans. When sticking out a shoot you have to absorb all the facts as they are, and try to think like a pheasant. For quality birds the further back the sticks are placed the better. One or two are bound to be lost out of the flanks but if good birds are wanted this is the only way — and there is always another day.

A decision cannot be made in a few minutes on the way to drive pheasants out of a wood. All the summer I would be studying the terrain and conditions to plan in my mind the best way to put it into operation. The only safe way to drive birds is to walk them

out quietly and drive them back to their home-ground.

As I travel around a lot of estates and witness shoots I always applaud the type of day where quality predominates quantity. I feel anything but elated when a big bag is made up with 'hedge-hoppers' — a good sporting day is not judged by the amount of game in the game larder.

I was second 'keeper at Raynham and it was no mean task to look after a load of beaters in the big woods. Some of the men I am sure came for a day out and a walk on the rides. I told them, "When you come and cut these rides you can have the privilege of walking on them!"

Occasionally we had an early morning duck shoot when we shot the lake out. The lake being situated in the low-lying ground at the front of the Hall, Batten and I planned a duck shoot for the next morning and he gave me instructions to walk the river down from East Raynham to the lake, which meant I would have to be up and walking the river half an hour before daybreak. The only thing I had to rely on for an early call was a rather unreliable alarm clock. Of course on this particular morning it failed to wake me and I suddenly awoke at six o'clock, jumped out of bed and said, "I'm supposed to be walking the river down." I grabbed my old bike, thinking all the time that there was only one thing for it, as I could hear the guns shooting in the distance, and that was to walk nonchalantly onto the scene as though I had been on the move for some time! I must confess this is what I did and much to my amazement, when I arrived, everybody was jumping about shouting "Great success, great success, some marvellous shots!" I never said a word but gave a wry smile, thinking somebody was on my side for once. We did buy another alarm clock though.

Always trying to make time to train dogs, I bought two well-bred black labrador pups, so whenever I had a spare minute, I took them out with me as I went about my duties, and in the evenings took them on the meadow near the house to put them through their paces. I took dogs in to train for other people, training them to their particular requirements. Jack Batten was a good man with a dog and we often downed tools when we were working to put the latest pup through its paces. When all the 'keepers got together, or we called on one another, there was always a display of dog-schooling.

While living there, I was introduced to a part of the North Norfolk coast which until then was unknown to me. George, the village grocer, took me fishing at Brancaster. We netted the creeks for flounders and dabs which I thoroughly enjoyed. Later on in the season we went to Morston, wildfowling. This became a regular occurrence and as soon as the weather was right, he gave me a call at any time of the night or day. I loved roaming the marshes; the remoteness and the bird life was a source of wonder to me. Thus began a long association with that part of the coast. Later on, after much scrimping and saving, we managed to buy an old car, it was an Austin Seven with a coupé hood. We paid thirty pounds for it, which seemed a small fortune to us in those days! The children were very excited at the prospect of having a ride in this funny little old car and nicknamed it 'The Gillie Cart.' Having transport made a lot of difference to our lives at Raynham, as we were able to get home to see our parents and take the children to a show occasionally. Also I was able to reach Morston under my own steam, where I was easily lured away to the creeks and the lovely Norfolk marshes. We began spending holidays there, year after year. Even after we left Raynham, we continued to return, teaching the boys to fish and swim and sail. When the tide was out, we went after cockles, and in the small pools, the boys went fishing with a piece of bacon-fat tied with a length of string. The small soft crabs which were easy prey with the bait caused great excitement for they soon had a bucket full. When the wind was right for wildfowling I was off down to the marshes before daylight or on an evening flight. We took up position on the high bank and laid low, waiting for the duck to come in. George and I always called in at the nearest pub, The Anchor, to sign in as we called it, or to let somebody know we were out on the marshes. When we returned, more often than not we were soaking wet through and we called in at The Anchor to dry out in front of a roaring fire and have a hot toddy. On my frequent visits to this part of the coast, I developed an interest in sea fishing which I took up later in life when gamekeeping wasn't so demanding.

We had a lot of enjoyment out of The Gillie Cart but sadly she got beyond repair. With the children now at school, Pauline took a part-time office job and we were able to save for something a little more reliable in the way of a rather smart Standard Twelve.

However I was beginning to feel that I would be Second Keeper at Raynham forever unless I seriously considered making a move. I decided to keep my eyes open for something better and daily scanned all the advertisements in the newspapers and shooting magazines. There was plenty of work available for an experienced 'keeper and I answered several adverts, but was very cautious when attending interviews as some of the situations were highly suspect. Some of the estates I went to were appalling: if there was a decent house, the job was not worth having or vice versa. I enjoyed the experience of working at Raynham and I know they didn't want me to leave. It was a privilege to work for Lord and Lady Townshend — whether on the estate or on other shoots, our welfare was always given their kind consideration. We lived at Mill Covert for six years but I felt that I couldn't condemn my wife and children to living in such an isolated place forever.

Eventually I contacted the Somerleyton estate which resulted in our saying farewell to West Norfolk and we were off back to Suffolk.

CHAPTER 8

Somerleyton Estate

Before my engagement as 'keeper at Somerleyton I had an interview with His Lordship, who spent a considerable amount of time showing me the estate and the extent of my beat. This included Fritton Lake, where I was to be employed as decoy-man, and also the surrounding pheasant beat.

The accommodation provided was a bungalow which was situated near the decoy, but unfortunately it was not modernized and had no electricity. This was a disappointment as I certainly liked the situation but we had made up our minds that we must have a modernized house. Ivan was twelve years old, Paul nearing ten and we were expecting our third child in May so we couldn't consider the house in its present condition. Eventually we came to an amicable arrangement where we would live in a vacant house in the village while the bungalow was modernized, which would take about six months.

We moved onto the estate in early March and lived at 'The Nook,' situated in the main street in the village. This was very convenient for Pauline as for the first time since we had been married, we had a telephone kiosk outside in the street and the local shop next door. Once we got ourselves established, we had a chance to survey our surroundings and we both realized this was an area of great natural beauty. We visited the Hall and viewed the gardens and as my duties took me all over the estate, I was very impressed. After the bleakness and harshness of West Norfolk, the surrounding countryside looked kind and gentle.

Work commenced almost straight away on The Lodge, which was to be our home at the decoy. This was situated amongst the trees at the Lound end of the lake and only about fifty yards away from the lake. The lake is surrounded by a vast area of woodland and in spring-time the foliage is very colourful, with the various shades of green supplemented by the rhododendrons and azaleas making splashes of vivid colour amongst the trees.

Our third son was born in early May and we named him Stephen. With the other boys being older, this new baby was made much of by all the family. But one blow we suffered with the expense of moving and a growing family was that we could no longer cope with the expense of running a car. We didn't consider the car a luxury, it was a necessity and to think we could no longer afford to run one didn't make us particularly happy. However it had to be sold and out came the old bike again. I had to cycle from the village, through Ashby, to my beat which wasn't very far but I then had to continue for a considerable distance to get round the beat.

There were four 'keepers employed at Somerleyton with Fred Ollett the Head Keeper. The estate had been well looked after, which became evident when I had the tunnel traps going to catch the vermin. I soon picked up the threads again and readily resumed a 'keeper's duties.

We moved into the bungalow at the decoy in early October and it looked very smart after it had been renovated. We still hadn't mains electricity but this problem was overcome by having a stationary diesel engine situated away from the house. It was fully automatic. When a light was switched on in the house, the engine started and generated the electricity and when the last light was switched off, it stopped. More often that not this would happen as it should, but on occasion, usually when it was raining hard, we would get ready for bed and when turning the last light off, the engine would remain running. Then I had to turn out in my night-clothes and turn the engine off manually. We were limited on output so we had a 'Rayburn' for cooking but used electricity for the washing machine, TV and ironing. The only drawback with this arrangement was that the engine seemed to use a colossal amount of fuel and was therefore very expensive to run. The bungalow was very snug and we soon had it comfortable. We had also moved at a convenient time of the year to prepare for the shooting season and to work the decoy.

The decoys on Fritton Lake, or 'pipes' as they were called, were situated at the Lound end of the lake. These pipes are inlets dug out at the edge of the lake to all points of the compass. In my day there were only two in operation, the other being derelict. The inlets which were covered by iron frames, shaped to half-hoops, were twenty-four feet across and twelve feet high at the entrance. These dimensions gradually narrowed down to one foot, forming a tunnel. There was a bend in the tunnel and the iron frame was covered with wire netting. On the small end of the pipe was a trammel net where the wildfowl congregated and were killed. The bend in the tunnel was concealed from the lake where the ducks were coyed. Reed screens were situated at various places near the pipes to conceal the decoy-man and his brown dog from the wild-fowl on the lake.

I fed at the entrance to the pipes, gently coying the wildfowl in to this area. Then the dog was encouraged to show himself beyond the screen and walk to the narrow end of the pipes. The ducks mobbed the dog, flying and swimming towards it and by this time they were half-way up the pipe. The decoy-man appeared and at a wave of a handkerchief, the startled ducks continued up

to the end of the pipe to their doom. After making a catch the decoy-man and dog walked on a concealed path back to the mouth of the pipes to show the dog again, which has the effect of settling and calming down the ducks that were left on the lake after all the commotion.

With only two pipes operating in my time I was rather restricted to their use. I often had to wait for a favourable wind which was the wind blowing from the trammel net to the mouth of the pipe. However this was a very effective way of killing vast quantities of wildfowl for commercial purposes. Years ago there were several of these pipes in East Anglia which, having plenty of waterways — The Broads, rivers, and marshes with large dykes, was a natural habitat for wildfowl. When there had been days of rain the waters flooded the marshes and if after the rain there was insufficient wind to turn the windmills, there were no means of draining the marshes, which resulted in whole areas of marshland being flooded for days, attracting thousands of wildfowl. Now that the windmill has been replaced by electric pumps, after a rain gallons of water pour from the marshes into the rivers at a very high speed and the marshes are now so well drained that the wildfowl are limited to areas where they can feed. All the decoys have gradually closed, and once closed, they are not allowed to re-open for commercial purposes. It was being frowned upon as indiscriminate killing of wildfowl and his Lordship decided to call it a day. I ran the pipes on Fritton lake for four years before their use was terminated.

I had wire catcher-pens on the lake, which I fed and it was very interesting to see the different species of duck which were caught — pochard, goldeneye, goosander and even an Eider duck were amongst the selection. These rare specimens were sent to a wildfowl sanctuary. I also had quite a few ringed duck. It was amazing the distance they travelled, some coming from Siberia, and how they all piled in when the weather was rough.

When the pipes were in operation the pathways leading through the wood to the pipes had to be swept clean of twigs and leaves to keep noise down to a minimum when approaching. The screens also had to be kept in good repair. In rough weather when the lake froze, ice breaking was a constant job, and meant being up early in the morning with an ice-pick to feed and water the wild-fowl before the duck flew in. The two main species to spend each summer on the lake were mallard and shelduck.

The mallard starts to lay her eggs in March. Anywhere suitable for the hen will do, under bushes, in the bracken, in a hollow tree — I have even found nests in a straw stack. The nest is made of feathers and down and the eggs kept covered with the same materials. When the hen sits, she pushes this all to one side of the nest to snuggle down on her eggs, and while sitting she keeps busy putting the feathers and down all over her back, the only thing visible being her head. On leaving the nest she lifts her body and on going forward flaps her wings to shed all the feathers and down on top of the eggs, leaving them camouflaged and covered until she returns.

The shelduck likes to get under the biggest rhododendron bush or into the biggest rabbit-hole she can find, to make her nest. These birds are very vicious at the best of times, especially when they are sitting and it pays to give them a wide berth. On hatching off she leads the chicks into the water and mothers them for five days. While she is busy with the chicks, the cock bird is in attendance in the background. After about five days or when the chicks are strong enough, the cock bird will commence flying backwards and forwards for short distances in a straight line. He keeps this up all the time while chatting to his mate. The hen assembles the brood of about twelve to fourteen chicks and proceeds with them trailed out behind. All the time the cock bird is acting as path finder, flying backwards and forwards telling her which direction to take. Walking for a considerable distance with these chicks, the cock directs them to salt water, such as Breydon Water near Great Yarmouth.

I ran the decoy for four seasons until His Lordship decided to call it a day and close it down. We would only shoot the lake during the season at appropriate times. This decision had disastrous results when it came to my livelihood. I was paid a bonus on the amount of duck that I caught and the feathers were a handy perk. Some of the feathers on the shoulders and flanks of the mallard drakes are used for making fishing flies. I collected all the feathers that were of use and sent them to the fur and feather merchants who paid up to one pound an ounce for some of them.

Apart from the lake, I had to attend to my pheasant beat. For pheasant rearing we pot nested, which consists of keeping all the clear eggs from the previous season and putting all the eggs in a bath with a layer of builder's lime in the bottom, then a layer of eggs, continuing in layers of lime and eggs with a final cover of lime. This was left to stand until the last week in March when we removed the eggs from the bath and gently cleaned them.

When walking in the wood, I looked for a sunny position underneath a briar to make a scrab or nest; upon completion I inserted three of the eggs marked with a cross. Making these scrabs in various places, about seventy-five in all, was to encourage the hen pheasants to use the nests.

Being bad mothers, they welcomed ready-made ones. By visiting the nests it was soon obvious which ones were struck. When the hen had laid three eggs we withdrew the pot eggs and destroyed them and then began a regular collection of eggs — it is not uncommon to have several hen birds laying in one nest — which were all taken to the rearing field. In a hut with a sanded floor we laid the eggs on the sand until we were ready to set them down. When we had sufficient eggs to meet our requirements we destroyed the nests, and subsequently the hens went their own way and made their own. This is quite an effective way of getting eggs and rearing from wild stock. By modern standards the only criticism is that this is a very time-consuming process. We then carried on rearing in the usual way, taking the birds out into the various coverts when they were six weeks old. Come the shooting season we had some very good pheasant and partridge days and I took with me to Somerleyton my experience of flying high pheasants which I knew His Lordship appreciated. I remember my first day's shooting at Somerleyton; we shot the home beat near the Hall and the gardens. Since arriving on the estate I had been confined more or less to my own beat. After the stand near the Hall, Ollett said, "There's a bird down over there," pointing in the direction of the gardens. I took the dog and went off and unknowingly entered the famous maze. From then on, after finding the bird, I seemed to spend a considerable amount of time trying to get out, until Ollett came to rescue me!

It had been hard work running the pheasant beat as well as the decoy but when this was closed, I had more time to put in on the beat, which improved no end over a period of time, resulting in me holding the record for the Ashby beat. It was very gratifying to put on a good show and I believe the record still stands at the present time. There was always keen competition between the 'keepers to outdo each other on shooting days. This led to hilarious baiting of one another. After putting on my good show Jack, the 'keeper on the home beat, congratulated me when we were hanging the game in the larder. He remarked, "I suppose you've had the old bottle out, Culley." He meant 'Indian Sweet Oils' which was sometimes used by 'keepers in the field to draw pheasants to where they want them. I replied, "Yes, I'm never without it." "Have you got it on you now?" he asked. Without answering I reached in my pocket for a small bottle and offered it to him. "Is this the stuff?" he exclaimed unscrewing the top. He had a good sniff, first one nostril and then the other. He then gagged, and said, "What revolting stuff! What, does this draw pheasants?" I said, "Well, as you can see, it's done the trick today." He then had another sniff and exclaimed, "Phew!", Then handed me the bottle back. I replaced the bottle in my pocket. Presently the Head Keeper appeared and asked, "Frank, have you got the specimen from the dog that is ill? I'm calling to see the vet." I took the same bottle from my pocket and handed it to him. You should have heard the remarks after this episode! Though we had our individual beats, we all had to work together in the rearing season. Sometimes when there was a lull in the activities during the day, we had a little clay pigeon shoot on our own. I would throw up a rotten pheasant egg for the others to take a shot at. We had a contest on how many we could 'kill.' It took me to say, "Right, two bob on the next round," then unbeknown to the others, I threw a wooden dummy egg!

One afternoon when I was working at the edge of the lake repairing the reed screens, I saw a rowing boat making its way up the lake and entering the decoy part which was private. There was my sign telling any would-be trespassers, NO BOATING BEYOND HERE. The occupant came past the sign, still oblivious to its message. I whistled and called but he still kept coming into the decoy. I impatiently dropped my tools and made my way around the lake to accost my trespasser. I called again but he still took no notice. When I approached him I pointed to the sign but he just shrugged his shoulders. By this time I was beginning to lose patience. I grabbed hold of the stern of the boat and gave it a shove and said, "Get to hell out of here, you are disturbing my ducks." He then understood and said in broken English, "I no speak English but I understand you get plenty mad," and off he went rowing away back down the lake. The next day still feeling rather annoyed and not intending to let the matter drop, I cycled to the other end of the lake where the fishing boats are hired from. I complained at length to Billy about the trouble I had had with one of his customers and he said, "I know who you mean, he's the knife-thrower at Yarmouth circus!" After that statement I backed down and thought I had had a lucky escape.

When Stephen was about eighteen months old, we were able to purchase an ex-Post Office van. I paid forty-five pounds for this Morris van, I put it through the road test and then painted it blue with a brush and a pot of paint. We were all elated that we had transport again. It made such a difference for shopping as we were still miles from anywhere. The boys named it Betsy, and we certainly had our money's worth out of her. Once again we loaded cot, pram, dog, children and all the paraphernalia for a fishing holiday, into Betsy and roared off up to Morston for a well-earned holiday. I think this old van was everybody's god-send. At this time none of the other 'keepers had transport. We all piled in and off to the annual 'keepers' clay pigeon shoot at Cambridge where the usual good day was enjoyed by all, everyone trying to win the cup which always seemed to elude us.

We had several visitors while we lived at The Lodge. People called who were on holiday in the area to see the decoy. Even after it had closed, many requested to see it, being interested in its use. Also, any 'keeper's house seems to attract people who are interested in shooting or wildlife and our door was always open to people who dropped in.

One old boy who lived locally and used to visit us for a chat, bought himself a moped. He said he was on holiday the next day and was off to Gorleston on his machine to have a hair-cut. I said, "Well just be careful of the traffic lights in the centre of town when you go up the High Street. Only if the lights are on green can you go straight over." "Right-o, Frank," he replied. When I saw him again he gave me a telling off, "I got pulled up by the police when

I went up the High Street," he said, "I did as you said when I went up the street. The lights were on green so I went straight over, I had a hair-cut and a couple of pints. When I came back a policeman stopped me and said to me, 'You now came over those lights while they were on red.' I told him, 'What do you mean? They were green when I went up there!'" Then wagging a finger at me he said, "You never told me they changed!"

Other visitors were the gypsies. I found they would pull up on a nice grass verge anywhere on my beat. This involved several living-vans, old cars and several running dogs. These people were a real headache to me and I was always after them to move on. Sometimes I thought I had succeeded, only to find them in another leafy lane on another part of my beat. I had to let them stay one night, then I was after them to move on. I got very used to their tales as to why they couldn't move and before I got there I would be anticipating all the different reasons why they had to stay. A favourite one was, "Can't move today, Govnor', the wife's having a baby!" They never said when she was having a baby. They would let the wind out of the tyres of the van and say they had a puncture. The truth of the matter was that the wives left early in the morning to work on the beaches in Great Yarmouth, telling fortunes and selling their charms, leaving the men behind to hold the fort. I very often had to get the assistance of the local policeman to get them moved, if only for a short time.

Ivan took to freshwater fishing and would spend hours down by the lake with a rod and line. I also took him 'babbing' for eels on the warm sultry nights during the summer which he enjoyed. Both Ivan and Paul baited eel traps which they inspected before going to school in the mornings. Once when they went to inspect their trap, they retrieved two of the biggest eels I had ever seen. They weighed eleven pounds the two, which caused a lot of excitement at the time. I ran them into the market to the jellied eel stall where I asked the owner if he would like to purchase two eels. He said he wasn't particularly interested in buying eels, but when he saw the size of them, he immediately wanted to know if we could get some more that size. He paid the boys fifteen shillings which was quite a lot of money in those days.

As it was some eight years since myxomatosis had arrived, the rabbits were beginning to build up again and although the disease struck every autumn, an increasing number were becoming immune. Rabbit damage began to flare up and it was obvious something had to be done. His Lordship gave us the rabbits for the killing so I was back to the old days of controlling the rabbit population. Here again we bought ferrets and made snares, and as soon as the shooting season was over, we were bolting rabbits and all my fancy rabbit shooting came to light from my experiences at Moreton Hall. As we were getting the rabbits under control, we noticed some very unwelcome visitors. The estate was situated on an island and had never had fox trouble but during a very bad winter in 1963, the river froze and we noticed foxes beginning to put in an appearance. Several earths were scrabbed out and since then foxes have become well established. Also during this very cold spell, the lake froze over to a considerable depth. When shooting, we crossed the lake on foot and once there were twelve cars parked in the middle. A Land Rover was giving toboggan rides up and down the lake, much to everybody's amusement.

This inclement weather was a very bad time for the wildfowl — they came in their thousands for shelter. It also had disastrous effects on the wildlife. Those hit the hardest were the fish-eating birds like the kingfisher and heron. The cormorant could go to sea but the kingfisher was really badly hit by these arctic conditions. When I first went to Fritton, kingfishers were in abundance, sitting on the posts and bare branches around the lake. They are few and far between today — they took a setback in that terrible winter and I believe pollution has also taken its toll on the small fish that these birds feed on.

As the boys were getting older we decided to leave Somerleyton. We loved our cosy bungalow but after the decoy closed, I suffered quite a drop in my earnings. I began to look around at people employed in industry and other jobs and I became rather dissatisfied with trying to provide for a family on gamekeepers' wages. I decided to quit gamekeeping for good, though I was told at the time by The Dowager Lady Somerleyton that I would never be able to give it up. Her Ladyship was right, I gave it a rest for two years, then I gradually worked my way into it again. It is the type of life you can never really give up; as you walk the countryside your eyes never miss what they are trained to see. Somerleyton is one of the most beautiful estates I have had the pleasure to work on and all the family thoroughly enjoyed living there.

CHAPTER 9

A Keeper's Observations

Dogs have always been of great interest to me. I have taken them in for training for several people. Usually I had two of my own, my old bitch from whom I was inseparable and one to train and sell. Gamekeepers' wages are not the best and these little sidelines helped to supplement the pay.

Being interested in dogs, I always observed the behaviour of other people's dogs in the shooting field. More often than not it is not the dog's fault when it misbehaves. Owners seem to spend a lot of money and use my valuable time to make sure their dog is trained correctly, only to let it get out of hand after a few months. I always think that after spending so many patient hours training a dog, it's worth a little time to train the owner. To have a dog obey your every command is truly an asset in or out of the shooting field. An ill-behaved child reflects on his parents and it is the same with dogs and their owners.

I have witnessed some funny experiences in my time regarding dogs. One gun stopped at my house, got out of his car, pulled the old dog out and proceeded to give him a walloping. When I questioned, "Has the dog done something wrong?" he replied, "No, but he jolly well soon will do, and I won't be able to catch him!"

Another gun let his labrador out of the car about five miles before he reached the shoot. On being asked why, he said, "He is just about ready for a day's shooting by the time he gets here!"

One gentleman carried a side-bag containing a length of chain, hammer and stake. At every stand he proceeded to hammer in the stake, and chain up the dog until after the drive. When he wanted the dog to retrieve, he released him, resulting in the dog charging all over the place. With great difficulty he caught him, giving a repeat performance at the next drive.

My favourite dog was a black labrador. I have had some wonderful dogs in my time but Major was the best I ever had. I had him from a puppy and trained him up to field-trial standard. He responded to my whistle and hand signals in an instant. I sold him for one hundred pounds in the 'fifties, a lot of money in those days.

I had some amazing mongrels for rabbiting, one of which was a half-bred Irish water-spaniel bitch. Really, she was a pet for the children. However, on hearing the gun click, Penny invited herself along to a day's rabbiting. When I roughed-up a hedge and there was a rabbit inside she pointed to it. I directed her with a hand movement to go through the fence and come in from the other side. By doing this she drove the rabbit out to my side, then I could shoot it. I never gave any commands, Penny knew what to do.

Sherry, a whippet-cross-labrador was the same, she anticipated my every moment. When I was bolting rabbits, she sat by the ferret box completely unconcerned, but taking it all in. But as soon as a rabbit was wounded she had it, and when I took the ferret box into a wood to start rabbiting, Sherry started sniffing in all the holes to tell me where the rabbits were. When I turned the ferret in, she listened, then went to the spot and started scratching where I was to start digging. While I was digging she took up position at the bolt hole, ready to make a grab should the rabbit bolt.

Getting up at daybreak is an ideal time to observe the birds and animals. When it is a fine sunny morning, every animal likes to greet the day. Getting right for the wind and concealing myself,

I have had some very entertaining times watching animals at play, foxes especially. About the middle of March the dog fox and vixen will hunt around to prepare their earths, until maybe they have prepared four or five. To know which one they are going to use, you have to wait and keep your eye on them. When they finally select an earth, you know they are there to stay and can observe them from a distance as it's fatal to get too close — they will know you have been around.

When the vixen has had her cubs, she will stay with them until they are ten days old, then she moves out, coming back at night to feed them. I have had to dig several earths out in my time. There are five or six entrances to an earth. In the centre is the main chamber which is where the vixen will lay with her cubs. One of the entrances does not carry through to the main chamber but is stopped off with a partition of earth and this space is used for a larder. All the time the vixen is inside with the cubs, the dog fox deposits his catch in the larder. The catch consists of rats, rabbits, pheasants, chickens and ducks. I have even found a lamb. When the vixen wants to feed while she is mothering the cubs, or to tempt the cubs onto solid food, she scrabs the earth away at the partition and enters the larder. The food she takes out is the first deposited, being about two weeks old, green and mellow. They prefer this to freshly killed meat. After feeding the cubs she then assists the dog in stocking the larder. On digging out a larder I have found a variety of animals but I have never found a mole amongst the collection. I have observed the foxes playing with a mole in the same way as a dog. A fox likes plenty of company around the earth. They seem to ignore rabbits when they are bobbing about near their home. I have been amazed to see them playing with pheasants on a ride. When I have noticed this, I usually have a good look round as sometimes you get cubs three-quarters grown, living on top in the undergrowth. Most probably the vixen has been

disturbed from her earth and they are laying rough. If this little party gets near the tame pheasants they will certainly trim them out.

I have had farmers come after me when they have been troubled with foxes raiding their chickens. I would have a good look around and follow the foot prints which went all over the place, finishing up in the centre of a ploughed field and there were the chickens, half buried in just a little scrab. The foxes came back later, usually about two weeks later unless they got short of food.

Sometimes when I have been going across a meadow to feed the birds, I have noticed the cow-pats have all been turned over. I knew then that Foxy had been about, looking for the big old black beetles which they love — I think they have them for dessert! This is the most rewarding part of my profession, to walk in the woods and take note of all the signs. A lot of people are born and bred in the country but never see the wood for the trees. I suppose I am naturally observant of these things and these instincts are put to good use in the country. There is a reason for every minute thing that is awry in the countryside.

When making comparisons between my early days and the present time, the farms of today seem like dead places. I am a countryman bred and born from generations of country folk. The farms of yesteryear had the horses, cattle, sheep and fowl and all abounded with wildlife, from the birds to the bees. They also had the sweat and toil, spindly crops and poor living conditions for the farm worker. One great advantage in this modern age is the high technology with plant breeding. Fields of corn all uniform in height and yield, with not a weed in sight, is a marvellous achievement, and yields of over three tons an acre are enough to make the old farmers turn in their graves.

Unfortunately, there is always a price to pay for progress and most things are reckoned by trial and error, and I believe the landowners and farmers are slowly beginning to realize the error of their ways. In my opinion all this high technology is no excuse for the vanishing hedgerows. I know with large machinery the fields are easier to negotiate — larger fields may be necessary but not so as to reduce our countryside into a prairie.

As I have mentioned previously, remembering my poaching days, the pit hole, or little old whistle hole as we called them, gave cover to the birds in rough weather and were a little haven for all sorts of wildlife. Most of these have been filled in, resulting in all this natural cover disappearing.

We cannot put the clock back to the olden days, we must have change which is all part of progress, for we all have to make a living, but with a little bit of compromise on the part of the farmer and landowners in this over-producing age, I am sure an amicable balance could be achieved. For a start, apart from the woodlands, if every farmer gave one per cent of his acreage to undisturbed conservation, perhaps the wildlife would have a little gain. When I say undisturbed, I mean an area permanently set aside for this purpose. Even if this desirable arrangement could be reached, I don't think I will ever see the English partridge coming back to strength without intensive rearing. The sprays have taken their toll on the insects and larvae, the mainstay of their diet.

All these actions in the countryside have far-reaching effects. Back in the late nineteen-fifties, we had the outcry of "Ban the gin-trap." This was a barbarous tool, but very effective and would probably be in use today if left to the professionals. I consider it as not as barbarous as myxomatosis which I think was diabolical, and still is, when you compare the long and lingering death by myxomatosis with the short effective one of the gin-trap.

I have witnessed considerable rabbit damage in my time, but the rabbit population can be contained, providing food and employment. There is an old saying when sowing seeds, 'One for the cook, one for the crow, one to rot and one to grow.' Like every other animal, rabbits have their part to play in the balance of nature and everything and everybody has got to live. The rabbit was not only food for us, but food for the stoats, weasels and other animals and birds of prey. Coming back to the gin-trap, I hope I never see rabies visit these shores. The fox would be the biggest carrier of this disease as he is so elusive and the only effective way of catching foxes is with the gin. Since the gin has been banned, the fox population has increased immensely. Snares are still legal provided they have a stop but according to reports, this is not very effective. The place to snare foxes is where they track through a hole in the fence. If all the hedges are removed, where do you snare them? We hear of foxes coming into the towns, raiding dustbins and coming into contact with domestic animals — years ago this was unheard of. This shows that their numbers have increased and that there has been no effective substitute for the gin-trap.

Where have all the red squirrels gone? I haven't seen one for years, the grey squirrel has taken over. It comes back to control again. Where are all the mice and voles that provide feed for the owls? Where is the variety of birds in the countryside? There are more in the towns than in the country and almost the only survivor is the humble sparrow. Even the poor bats cannot find enough insects to keep theselves alive. All these problems are man-made and surely man can solve them. We must have more areas of conservation.

Coming back to gamekeeping, on one of the estates I was on, during the week before Christmas, we had the Christmas shoot. Most of the pheasants that were shot were presents for the tenant farmers and professional people on the estate. A few days after the shoot we were summoned by the Head Keeper to distribute the game to the various people on our individual beats. The pheasants were all tied in a brace with tickets showing who they were for. The Head Keeper gave me my load plus another brace, saying "Take this brace to the parson. I have been taking him a brace for years and I've never had a drink out of him so you might as well take them!" "Typical," I thought!

I went on my rounds and delivered the birds to the tenant farmers, getting a couple of bob here and there, and a drink. Arriving at the Rectory I rang the bell. The vicar opened the door and I held out the pheasants to him and said, "Here you are." He took them in this hand but looking rather disconcerted, he said, "My dear man, that isn't the way to deliver a present from His Lordship. Let me show you. Step inside and you be the rector and I will be the gamekeeper." Having had a few drinks already, I was game for anything. I stepped inside, closed the door and waited for him to ring the bell. When he rang the bell I opened the door, he handed me the pheasants and said, "Good Morning, sir, here is a brace of pheasants with the compliments of His Lordship. A Merry Christmas." I promptly replied, "Thank you 'keeper, come in and have a drink!"

I have met some wonderful characters on my travels and have thoroughly enjoyed most of my experiences. There is a saying amongst 'keepers '364 days' work for one day's disappointment!' This very often happens, you plan all the year for a big day, you are full of optimism when you start off but things don't always go right, then you feel deflated. But when everything does go right — a lovely bright frosty morning, the dogs full of expectancy, the beaters with their lively chatter, good birds, good guns and everybody having a good day, it makes it all worthwhile.

Having been involved with shooting for most of my life it gives me great pleasure to have such a day. There is only one thing which I cannot tolerate and that is when guns swing round when shooting and shoot at birds going away from them, when very often they could have been shot in front. Nearly all the wounded birds are shot going away and if this rule was observed, it would cut the wounded down to a minimum. A wounded bird is no good to anybody, it only causes unnecessary suffering.

These are my observations; I hope they are of interest to the reader. Now I am retired I can break all the rules and have an old cat lying on the hearth. He is the biggest poacher, whichever side of the fence he strolls . . . . .